Legal Writing in Context

Legal Writing in Context

Sonya G. Bonneau
Professor of Legal Research and Writing
Georgetown Law

Susan A. McMahon
Professor of Legal Research and Writing
Georgetown Law

Carolina Academic Press
Durham, North Carolina

Library of Congress Cataloging-in-Publication Data

Names: Bonneau, Sonya G., author. | McMahon, Susan A., author.
Title: Legal writing in context / Sonya G. Bonneau and Susan A. McMahon.
Description: Durham, North Carolina : Carolina Academic Press, LLC, 2017.
Identifiers: LCCN 2017021736 | ISBN 9781611635218 (alk. paper)
Subjects: LCSH: Legal composition | Law--United States--Methodology.
Classification: LCC KF250 .B66 2017 | DDC 808.06/634--dc23
LC record available at https://lccn.loc.gov/2017021736

e-ISBN 978-1-5310-0871-0

CAROLINA ACADEMIC PRESS
700 Kent Street
Durham, North Carolina 27701
Telephone (919) 489-7486
Fax (919) 493-5668
www.cap-press.com

Printed in the United States of America

Contents

Acknowledgments

Many, many people provided thoughtful feedback and advice on this book. First and foremost, thanks to the students who contributed invaluable research assistance: Jamin Agosti, Joel Nolette, and Lijun Zhang. Special thanks to Lijun for his editing and Bluebooking prowess as we finalized the book.

Thanks also to our Georgetown Law colleagues, especially Erin Carroll, Rima Sirota, and Jarrod Reich, who gave wise feedback on earlier versions of the work. Georgetown Law generously provided research support to assist in the completion of the book, for which we are enormously grateful.

We have presented various chapters at conferences over the past few years, and many thanks to the attendees at the Capital Area Legal Writing Conference at the University of the District of Columbia, the Association of Legal Writing Directors Conference at the University of Memphis, and the Legal Writing Institute Conference in Portland, Oregon, for their thoughtful questioning of some of the approaches we take in these pages. Thanks to Carolina Academic Press for working with us from start to finish and being so responsive to our ideas.

Last but certainly not least, we thank our families for their support during the years-long process of completing this book. Susan is especially grateful to Tom Spoth, the best copy editor/husband a girl could ask for. Sonya has extra thanks for her husband Bob, who provided encouragement, humor, and tech support, and for Charlotte, her favorite kid.

Prologue

In this text, you will learn to think deductively and analogically. You will learn to distill the holdings of multiple cases into a coherent legal rule. You will learn to craft a compelling narrative. You will learn how legal rules can sometimes (but not always) control the outcome of cases, and how to argue for an outcome when the legal rules provide no answers.

All of these ideas have rich and deep theoretical groundings. You will learn those foundations, too, because to practice law brilliantly and eloquently is to adopt new approaches and present new lines of thought. To be effective and creative, you must know why the approaches to reasoning and communication we advocate here work. That will help you to know when deviation from those approaches is justified.

To teach you these foundations, we have mined the writings not only of our fellow legal writing professors, but also legal theorists, cognitive psychologists, and philosophers. The end result (we hope) is a book that not only provides a guide to effective legal reasoning and communication, but also shows *why* the suggestions made in this book work well (and notes where others may disagree with the strategies set forth here).

A good lawyer can apply well-established legal rules to new sets of facts. A great lawyer can advocate for the evolution of those rules and recognize when a changing society requires a new approach. This book's aim is to teach you to be good, and set you on the path to being great.

Legal Writing in Context

Unit 1

Law and Legal Reasoning

This unit introduces you to the intricacies of reasoning like a lawyer. Many newcomers to the legal profession (like first-year law students) toil under the misapprehension that becoming a lawyer means memorizing the law. Yet no student graduates law school knowing the entirety of legal doctrine—that universe is simply too large—and any effort to do so is futile, as the law can (and likely will) change in the future.

Instead, the goal of law school is to give you the reasoning tools that you can use to solve any legal problem you face. In most classes, you learn to think like a lawyer through osmosis; it runs through the discussions in Contracts or Property like an underground river. This book aims to bring that secret well-spring to the surface by introducing the kinds of reasoning that lawyers most commonly engage in. And at the core of legal reasoning is the application of an enforceable legal rule to a set of facts.

Let us begin with a simple example of legal reasoning in practice. Cars must stop at red lights. Why? Because a local statute requires this action. That statute is the legal rule; the fine you may receive for running a red light is the enforcement of the legal rule. Between the rule and the enforcement of the rule is legal reasoning, or the application of the legal rule to specific factual circumstances to determine an outcome.

If the statute simply says "All cars must stop if the light turns red before the cars enter the intersection," the legal rule to be applied is clear. When the light has turned red, and the car proceeds through the intersection, the factual circumstances obviously fall within the boundaries of that rule. A driver who does this usually gets a ticket.

But, in many cases that come to a lawyer's office, either the legal rule is inherently ambiguous or the application of the legal rule to the facts of a specific case is ambiguous. For example, the statute may allow a driver to "turn right on red if it is possible to safely do so." This legal rule is ambiguous because it gives discretion to the enforcer of the rule. A safe right turn into oncoming traffic for an average driver may not be safe for an extremely slow one. And one enforcer's notion of a safe distance between cars may radically differ from a more risk-averse enforcer's notion. The outcome in this case is not as clear-cut.

Even when the legal rule is not inherently ambiguous, e.g., "stop when the light turns red," it can become so when applied to a particular factual context. Let's say a car is just before the stop line when the light turns red and the driver cannot safely halt the car. He continues through the intersection. Has the driver run the red light? Or what if a motorist is rushing her husband to the hospital and can safely cross the intersection; is there an implicit exception to the stop-on-red rule in emergencies? The enforcer of the legal rule must make that judgment because the rule itself does not explicitly address these scenarios; again, the outcome is uncertain.

Much of a lawyer's work takes place in that ambiguous space between the legal rule and the enforcement of the rule. To think like a lawyer is to find the legal texts that address the unresolved question and reason from those texts to a resolution. Often, there is no one correct answer; what counts is not the answer you reach, but the strength of your reasoning.

The chapters to come will provide insights into how to find the texts that address the relevant legal question and use those sources to craft sturdy and convincing legal analysis.

Chapter 1

Sources of Law

To apply a legal rule, one must first know where to find it. This chapter introduces both the sources of law and the relative weight of those sources.

Within the American legal system, a multitude of government entities promulgate legal rules. First, both the federal government and state governments can enact and enforce laws within their particular zone of authority. Second, each government has a variety of institutions responsible for promulgating law. The legislative and executive branches traditionally craft statutes and regulations, respectively, while the courts both interpret those authorities and develop the common law.

From this field of legal authorities, an attorney must pluck those rules that best determine the outcome in a particular case. To do so effectively, she needs a solid grasp of which authorities bind the court deciding the issue and which ones merely persuade. To bind a court means that the court must follow the decision of another government institution, even if the judge strongly disagrees with that decision. To persuade a court means that the court may adhere to the prior decision of a government institution, but is not required to do so.

To be binding, a legal authority must be promulgated by an entity and in a form that govern the deciding court. Attorneys use a kind of decision tree—called the hierarchy of authority—to determine whether a given piece of law is binding or persuasive. We discuss how to reach these conclusions in the sections below.

A. Hierarchy of Legal Authorities

Legal rules in the federal system usually come from one of four main sources: constitutions, statutes, regulations, or judicial decisions.[1] State governments largely track this structure.

Rules originating in each of these sources do not have the same weight. For example, the federal government cannot enact a statute that conflicts with a provision of the U.S. Constitution. If it does, the statute is invalid.[2] And a legislature may overturn a judicial decision by passing a statute that is contrary to the court's decision.[3] The hierarchy of these authorities is represented visually here, and each type of authority is explained in more detail below.

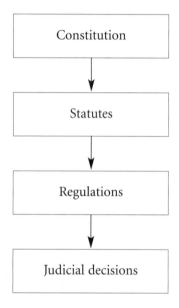

---

1. Other sources of law in the federal system include treaties, executive orders, administrative agency decisions, and court rules. These sources can be quite important for attorneys practicing in particular subject-matter areas, but are beyond the scope of this introduction.

2. *See, e.g.*, Marbury v. Madison, 5 U.S. 137, 177–80 (1803) (holding that if an act of the legislature is repugnant to the Constitution, then courts have authority to invalidate the act); United States v. Eichman, 496 U.S. 310, 318–19 (1990) (invalidating the Flag Protection Act of 1989 because it conflicts with the First Amendment of the U.S. Constitution).

3. *See, e.g.*, Lilly Ledbetter Fair Pay Act of 2009, Pub. L. No. 111-2, 123 Stat. 5 (codified at 42 U.S.C. §§ 2000a, 2000e-5). That said, there is quite a bit of complexity in the interplay between statutes and judicial decisions, as courts have the power to interpret statutes and declare them unconstitutional. The nuances of that interaction are beyond the scope of this chapter; for further reading on the topic, see generally Matthew R. Christiansen & William

1. Constitutions

A constitution is the founding document of a government. It is the source of a sovereign's power to promulgate legal rules, and it is itself a source of legal rules. A constitution thus lays out both the structure of government (such as the division of the federal government into three branches with separate powers[4]) and some of the laws of the jurisdiction (such as the prohibition on slavery within the United States[5]). The federal government cannot make a law inconsistent with the federal Constitution; the same principle holds for state governments and their constitutions. Thus, constitutions sit atop the hierarchy of legal authorities.

Despite their primacy, constitutions are often infuriatingly vague. For example, the Fourteenth Amendment of the U.S. Constitution prohibits any state from denying a person within its jurisdiction "the equal protection of the laws." Much judicial and scholarly ink has been spilled attempting to explain what that phrase means and how it should be measured. Moreover, a constitution leaves much of the work of crafting law to the legislature it has created. The U.S. Constitution's focus is generally on establishing limits on government power rather than promulgating specific legal rules.

Statutes, regulations, and common law have filled in the gaps between the general principles of a constitution and the nuts-and-bolts rules of a functional society.

2. Statutes

The legislature is primarily responsible for crafting statutes.[6] A statute is a codified legal rule that permits, requires, or prohibits activity. The legislature can pass a statute governing any activity within its sphere of authority (as set out in that sovereign's constitution). Thus, the U.S. Congress has passed statutes on a wide range of topics, from prohibiting Americans from bribing foreign officials[7]

N. Eskridge, Jr., *Congressional Overrides of Supreme Court Statutory Interpretation Decisions, 1967–2011*, 92 Tex. L. Rev. 1317 (2014); Deborah A. Widiss, *Shadow Precedents and the Separation of Powers: Statutory Interpretation of Congressional Overrides*, 84 Notre Dame L. Rev. 511 (2009); William N. Eskridge, Jr., *Overriding Supreme Court Statutory Interpretation Decisions*, 101 Yale L. J. 331 (1991).

4. U.S. Const. arts. I–III.

5. U.S. Const. amend. XIII.

6. Under Article I of the U.S. Constitution, the U.S. Congress passes legislation, and the President has the power to veto those bills before they become law. U.S. Const. art. I, §7.

7. Foreign Corrupt Practices Act of 1977, Pub. L. No. 95-213, 91 Stat. 1494 (codified as amended at 15 U.S.C. §§78m, 78l, 78dd-1, 78dd-2).

to instituting a system of health care across the country.[8] The U.S. Code is the collection of statutes passed by Congress; states have similar compilations. The work of legislative bodies has grown tremendously in recent years, and statutes now govern many areas of life. When researching an area of law, look first to see if a statute controls the outcome.

Much of the work of federal and state courts is consumed by statutes. When deciding a case involving a statute, a court does one of two things: (1) it attempts to discern the meaning of ambiguous provisions in the statute or its application to a set of facts, or (2) it determines whether the statute conflicts with the governing constitution and thus is void. Because constitutions trump statutes, any part of a statute that is deemed unconstitutional is no longer in effect.

We will discuss statutory interpretation in depth in Chapter Three.

3. Regulations

Regulations are rules issued by administrative agencies. A legislature often passes a statute that lays out the generalities of the conduct being permitted, required, or prohibited, but leaves the details of how the law is to be enforced or applied, or the specific procedures to be used, to the expertise of an administrative agency that specializes in that subject area. These agencies, which are part of the executive branch of government, then provide detail and heft to the statute through regulations. Federal regulations can be found in the Code of Federal Regulations; states have similar publications where their rules and regulations are compiled.[9]

Administrative agencies can exceed their grant of authority from the legislature in the regulations they write. Just as with statutes, courts can determine whether an agency's regulation exceeds its statutory authority.[10] If it does, the regulation is set aside.

4. Judicial Opinions

It may surprise you to see judicial opinions at the bottom of this hierarchy. After all, courts have the power to tell both the executive and legislative

---

8. Patient Protection and Affordable Care Act, Pub. L. No. 111-148, 124 Stat. 119 (2010) (codified at 42 U.S.C. §§ 18001 et seq.).

9. See the state-by-state list at Cornell's Legal Information Institute for information on each state's administrative law regime. *See Listing by Jurisdiction*, LEGAL INFORMATION INSTITUTE, https://www.law.cornell.edu/states/listing (last visited Jan. 15, 2017).

10. 5 U.S.C. § 706(2)(C).

branches when they have overstepped their authority and can invalidate the rules they have written.

Courts also have the power to interpret ambiguous statutes and regulations. They can significantly modify those rules by adding a gloss of meaning to the language used. This interpretation of the texts adopted by the other branches of government is a large part of what courts do.

Yet courts are in many ways bound by the acts of legislatures and executive branches. A court can interpret a constitutional statute; it cannot override such a statute or create precedent that directly conflicts with the language of the statute. For example, a court is bound by a statute that states: "A driver must stop at a red light." It cannot hold that a driver who ran a light five seconds after it turned red did not violate the statute.[11]

In addition, courts are also rule-making bodies themselves, as many areas of law, known as common law, have developed solely through court decisions. Contracts, torts, and property are typical areas where courts have developed a significant body of law in the absence of any controlling statute. Yet the legislature has the power to overturn common law by passing a statute that conflicts with the common law.

Thus, courts are bound by these other sources of law. Yet a court system is not a single entity, like a legislature promulgating statutes or an administrative agency promulgating regulations. It is a linked network of courts issuing decisions, and some of those decisions conflict with one another. Within the court system, a hierarchy of authority determines which past decisions a court must follow. The next section outlines that hierarchy in more detail.

B. Hierarchy of Courts

Courts are bound by the decisions of courts that sit above them in the hierarchy. Thus, a federal district court must follow a precedent laid out by the appellate court in the same jurisdiction. Federal district and appellate courts must follow precedent from the U.S. Supreme Court.

---

11. As always, there are exceptions even to this rule. For example, if a driver was running a red light in order to get a dying man to the hospital, a court could potentially read into the statute an exception for such emergency situations. But if the driver ran a red light without any extenuating circumstances, then a court has no power to absolve him of his traffic ticket. In our discussion of statutory interpretation, we will further explore this conflict between clear statutes and ambiguous application of statutes to specific sets of facts.

This chain of command springs from the principle of *stare decisis*, Latin for "to stand by things decided." This institutional lodestar supports predictability, efficiency, and fairness in law by settling legal questions. Others can then rely on those decisions and adjust their behavior accordingly. The requirement that higher courts bind lower courts is known as vertical *stare decisis*, and it is considered absolute. Horizontal *stare decisis* refers to the principle that courts should follow their own past precedent, but it is a much more flexible proposition than vertical *stare decisis*.

This visual representation of the hierarchy represents the courts established by Article III of the U.S. Constitution. State governments largely track the same model, but some smaller states and the District of Columbia have only a trial court and then a court of last resort. The structure of appellate courts also varies from state to state. In the federal system and in some states, appellate courts bind only trial courts within their geographic jurisdiction; in other states, a ruling made in any appellate court binds all trial courts within the state.

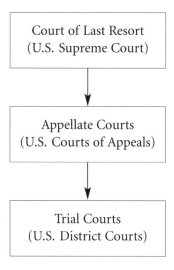

1. U.S. Supreme Court

In the federal system, the U.S. Supreme Court is the court of last resort. It binds all other federal courts and state courts deciding a question of federal law. The Supreme Court is bound only by itself under the concept of horizontal *stare decisis*. Unlike the vertical hierarchy of courts, this form of *stare decisis* is not an "inexorable command," and when circumstances render a prior holding unworkable, unjustifiable, or a "doctrinal anachronism," the Supreme Court can overrule a past case.[12]

The Supreme Court is made up of nine justices, and only majority opinions—those signed by five or more justices—constitute binding law. Concurrences with and dissents from the majority opinion may provide fodder for novel legal arguments, but they do not constrain the lower courts.

Not every part of a court decision (including those of the Supreme Court) is binding on lower courts. Opinions often contain both holdings and dicta. A holding is the resolution of the case. The holding and the reasoning that leads to the holding are binding on lower courts. Dicta are any statements in the opinion that are not necessary to the holding. The difference between holdings and dicta is often disputed; one clear example of dicta is when a court decides an issue on one claim, which resolves the case, but then speculates as to how it would decide a second claim if the first claim were not presented. In that circumstance, the court's decision on the first claim would bind lower courts, but its speculation as to how it would decide the second claim would not.

2. U.S. Courts of Appeals

The federal court system is divided into twelve geographic areas (called "circuits"), each of which has its own Court of Appeals. These courts hear appeals from the district courts within their jurisdiction.[13] For example, the U.S. Court of Appeals for the Fourth Circuit only hears appeals from the U.S. District Courts in Maryland, North Carolina, South Carolina, Virginia, and West Virginia. Appellate courts are made up of between ten judges (in the First Circuit) and twenty-nine (in the Ninth Circuit), but a panel of three randomly selected judges usually hears a particular case.

The panel's majority decision binds both the district courts in its jurisdiction and future three-judge panels in that circuit. The district courts are bound by vertical *stare decisis*; they must follow the precedents of the appellate court. Subsequent panels on the appellate court are bound by a form of horizontal *stare decisis* known as the law of the circuit. This form of horizontal *stare decisis*

---

12. *See, e.g.,* Planned Parenthood of Southeastern Pa. v. Casey, 505 U.S. 833, 854–55 (1992).

13. There is also the U.S. Court of Appeals for the Federal Circuit, which hears appeals on certain subject matters. For a map of the federal circuit courts, see generally *Court Role and Structure*, US Courts.gov, http://www.uscourts.gov/about-federal-courts/court-role-and-structure (last visited Jan. 15, 2017).

is much more rigid than that practiced by the Supreme Court; many circuits have some variation of the rule that a subsequent panel is bound by the holding of a previously published decision in that circuit.[14]

But a circuit court can overrule itself: A party who loses on appeal can petition the circuit court for a re-hearing *en banc*, which is a panel comprised of every judge who sits on that particular appellate court. An *en banc* decision can either uphold or overturn the majority opinion of the panel and then binds both subsequent appellate panels and the lower courts in that jurisdiction. Parties to a case do not have a right to an *en banc* hearing; a majority of the judges must agree to hear the case. These petitions are rarely granted, and an appellate court only takes on a case *en banc* if there is a split within the circuit or the question is one of "exceptional importance."[15]

3. U.S. District Courts

District courts are the starting point for cases in the federal court system. Each state and territory in the United States has at least one district court, and some have several (California, for example, has the Northern District of California, the Central District of California, and the Southern District of California). Within each district court are several judges. The Northern District of California, for example, has twenty-one Article III judges divided among three courthouses. Each case filed in a district court is assigned to a single judge, who handles the case from beginning to end. Judges usually do not sit on multi-member panels, as they do in the appellate courts.

A district court is the trial court in the federal system. Both the appellate courts and the Supreme Court hear arguments about what happened at the trial court, but only the district court collects evidence and hears from witnesses.

A district court is bound by the decisions of the appellate court within its jurisdiction and of the U.S. Supreme Court. District courts do not practice any form of horizontal *stare decisis*, so decisions of district courts do not bind the court itself or any other courts. Judges may find a decision of a district court colleague persuasive, but they are not required to defer to the decision.

---

14. *See* Joseph W. Mead, *Stare Decisis in the Inferior Courts of the United States*, 12 Nev. L.J. 787, 795 (2012). The rules governing the deference later panels give to earlier decisions vary considerably by circuit, and the Seventh Circuit arguably follows a less rigid *stare decisis* rule that allows one panel to overrule another. *Id.* at 794, 794 n.54. Also, generally only a panel's published decisions (i.e., decisions that are included in an official reporter) are considered binding; unpublished decisions are often given minimal consideration, although the treatment of unpublished decisions varies considerably by circuit. *See id.* at 798–99, 799 n.86.

15. Fed. R. App. P. 35(a).

C. State and Federal Systems

The sections above laid out the hierarchy of authority within a particular jurisdiction, but there are times when binding authority crosses jurisdictional boundaries. On occasion, federal courts are bound by state law, and state courts by federal law.

State law can end up in federal court in one of two ways. First, diversity jurisdiction: If the plaintiff and defendant come from different states and the damages at stake amount to more than $75,000, the plaintiff may bring his case in federal court.[16] Second, supplemental jurisdiction: If the plaintiff has both a federal law claim and a state law claim arising from the same set of factual circumstances, the plaintiff can often bring the claim in federal court.[17]

Federal law has a much less restricted path to state courts. State courts are courts of general jurisdiction, which means they can hear any claim, except for cases in which the United States is a party or cases over which federal courts have exclusive jurisdiction.[18] While federal courts can hear only cases in which there is some federal law or diversity jurisdiction hook, state courts can hear cases involving federal law alone (with the exception of cases involving statutes over which federal courts have exclusive jurisdiction), federal and state law, or state law alone.

When a federal court hears a case involving state law, or vice versa, it is bound by a different body of law than it would be if it were hearing a case with its own jurisdiction's law. For example, a federal court hearing a question of state law is bound by the decisions on that law from the highest court of that state. Thus, if the U.S. Court of Appeals for the Ninth Circuit were deciding a New York breach of contract claim, it would apply the New York Court of Appeals'[19] law on that issue to the facts of the case. But it is *only* the highest state court that binds the federal court. The decisions of New York state appellate courts would not technically bind the Ninth Circuit, but the circuit court would likely consider those decisions highly persuasive. If New York's

---

16. 28 U.S.C. § 1332.

17. 28 U.S.C. § 1367.

18. Federal courts have exclusive jurisdictions over cases involving specific federal laws: federal crimes, 18 U.S.C. § 3231; bankruptcy, 28 U.S.C. § 1334 (subject to certain exceptions); antitrust, 28 U.S.C. § 1337 (subject to certain conditions); copyright, 28 U.S.C. § 1338; patent, *id.*; and maritime cases, 28 U.S.C. § 1333.

19. The name of New York's highest court is the New York Court of Appeals, *Court of Appeals*, NYCourts.gov, http://www.nycourts.gov/courts/courtofAppeals.shtml (last updated Feb. 24, 2013), and its trial courts are called supreme courts, *Supreme Court*, NYCourts.gov, http://www.nycourts.gov/courts/cts-outside-nyc-SUPREME.shtml (last updated Feb. 9, 2015).

highest court has not ruled on the issue, then the federal courts will stand in the shoes of that court and attempt to predict what the state's highest court would do if faced with the case.

The same is true for federal law in state courts. The U.S. Supreme Court is binding on all courts on questions of federal law. When the New York Court of Appeals hears a case involving the First Amendment, the U.S. Supreme Court's law on that issue binds that state court, but the U.S. Court of Appeals for the Second Circuit's decisions on the First Amendment are merely persuasive.

D. Choosing among Persuasive Authorities

The task is usually not complete with the identification of binding authorities. Is there a single Supreme Court case that completely answers every question posed by your legal problem? If so, count yourself lucky. The vast majority of legal issues require a multitude of authorities to solve, and the binding authorities do not completely answer the question.

To fully analyze a legal problem, lawyers usually must also rely on persuasive authorities. A few factors influence how persuasive a particular authority is to a judge, but there is no clear defining line on what "the best" authority is. Attorneys learn to use their best judgment when selecting persuasive cases. Here are a few things to keep in mind, in roughly this order:

1. **Does the authority analyze the same (or a similar) legal rule?** A district court judge in the U.S. District of New Mexico is not bound by the decisions of her fellow district court judges. But she may look to them as a persuasive authority because those judges are operating under exactly the same binding precedent as she is. Similarly, a federal appellate court would look to the decision of another appellate court with similar law on a topic rather than to one on the other side of a circuit split.
2. **How analogous is the case?** Cases with facts deeply similar to the facts of the current issue provide the most compelling clues as to how a court might come down in this case. Provided that the law of the jurisdiction deciding the case is the same (or similar), factually analogous cases can prove highly persuasive.
3. **How well-reasoned is the decision?** A decision with impeccable logic and well-thought-through policy considerations is more likely to sway a decisionmaker than one that demonstrates only a cursory understanding of the issues at play.

4. **How many other courts have cited the decision favorably?** If the opinion has been cited again and again for the same point of law, then it has achieved some measure of respectability among judges. Follow the wisdom of crowds and consider using the case as well. (Keep in mind, though, that older cases enjoy an advantage here solely because of their age. Ensure that the case has not outlived its usefulness by also assessing the other factors above.)

5. **How old is the case?** A case from before the days of indoor plumbing will likely not hold much weight with a modern-day judge. But it may be useful despite its age if the law in the area has not changed and the facts are directly on point.

6. **Is the decision published?** Unpublished opinions carry less weight than published opinions.[20] Citation to unpublished opinions is highly disfavored in some jurisdictions. That said, a factually analogous, well-reasoned, recent unpublished opinion is a much more valuable resource than a dissimilar, cursory, old published opinion.

E. Secondary Sources

Other resources may shed light on a legal question, but are not sources of law. These "secondary sources" include treatises, legal encyclopedias, law review articles, restatements, and the like.[21] They comment on or collect the law, note larger trends, or provide insights into current legal thinking in a particular subject area. They are useful research tools, as they can provide an attorney with an overview of a particular area of law. Judges will also cite to these sources on occasion for a general point of law or in support of a novel argument that has little precedent. But the important thing to remember is that these resources are secondary; where an attorney has a binding primary source of law or a strong persuasive case, those sources are more compelling than a secondary source.

---

20. To be "published" means to appear in one of the official case reporters. Unpublished opinions do not appear in that hard-copy form, but are widely available on electronic databases.

21. For more information on each of these secondary sources, see Georgetown Law Library's Secondary Sources Research Guide, which is available at http://guides.ll.georgetown.edu/secondary.

Chapter 2

Procedure Overview

The last chapter walked you through the sources and hierarchy of legal authorities in the American system of government. The first step in any effective legal analysis is to develop a solid grasp of the binding and persuasive rules governing the outcome of your case.

The second step is to understand the scope of the legal problem you face. And in a litigation context, understanding the scope of the problem begins with understanding the procedural posture of your case.

What is procedural posture? It is the stage of the litigation. Whether you are at the very beginning of a case (perhaps advising a client before any complaint has been filed), in the middle (such as drafting a motion for summary judgment), or near the end (maybe filing a petition for certiorari to the Supreme Court), the procedural posture sets boundaries for the kinds of argument you can make and the kinds of facts you can use. By familiarizing yourself with the different boundaries for the different stages of a litigation, you will ensure that your analysis remains focused on relevant considerations.

Here are a few general guidelines: First, remember that the trial is the fact-finding portion of a case. Thus, if you are making a pre-trial motion, your factual arguments are usually quite circumscribed. Pre-trial motions typically focus on legal questions, not factual ones.[1]

Second, remember the different roles of the trial and appellate courts. A trial court's main task is to decide issues of fact in a particular case. An appellate

---

1. There are, of course, exceptions to this general rule. In criminal trials, for example, a judge often admits evidence, hears from witnesses, and decides factual questions on a motion to suppress evidence before a trial occurs. To determine whether the pre-trial motion you are making falls within the general "no fact-finding" rule or allows deeper consideration of factual questions, consult the procedural rules governing the motion.

court's main task is to determine issues of law for the entire jurisdiction. These institutional roles limit the kinds of decisions each court can issue.

With these general principles in mind, let's turn to the various stages of a civil trial and appeal and examine the boundaries set at each stage of the process.

A. Civil Trial

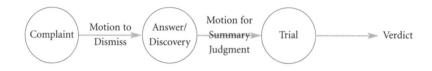

The above flowchart shows the common major stages of a federal civil trial. The text outside the circles represents a point at which a court could enter a final judgment. Once that judgment is entered, the losing party can appeal; you can thus think of each of these decision points as a potential place where the case could jump from trial court to an appeal.

1. Motion to Dismiss

A civil case in federal court begins when the plaintiff files a complaint, which must contain short and plain statements describing the grounds for jurisdiction, the claims, and a demand for the relief sought.[2] In response, a defendant may file an answer, which must admit or deny the allegations in the complaint and lay out any affirmative defenses.[3] Each claim must be admitted or denied; a failure to deny a claim may lead the court to conclude that the defendant has admitted it.[4]

Before filing an answer, a defendant has the option of filing a motion to dismiss. Rule 12 of the Federal Rules of Civil Procedure lays out several grounds for dismissal, but one of the most common is failure to state a claim upon which relief can be granted (Rule 12(b)(6)). To win on this motion, a defendant

---

2. FED. R. CIV. P. 8(a).
3. FED. R. CIV. P. 8(b)–(c).
4. FED. R. CIV. P. 8(b).

must argue that even if everything the plaintiff said in the complaint is true, the defendant still wins as a matter of law. The purpose of this motion is to weed out those cases that do not warrant incurring the lengthy and expensive discovery process because the complaint itself is fatally flawed.[5] To avoid a dismissal, the complaint need only show a plausible right to relief.[6]

This is a high bar for a defendant to achieve dismissal, and rightfully so. To eliminate more than the weakest cases would be to risk closing the courthouse doors in the face of parties who have a valid claim to be decided.[7] One common argument at this stage is that the plaintiff has not laid out enough factual support for his legal claims, e.g., in a contract case, he neglects to allege that the defendant made an offer which the plaintiff accepted. Another is that the plaintiff simply cannot win on the law. For example, a plaintiff alleges in his complaint that a defendant failed to murder a third party after the defendant signed a contract to do so; the defendant could argue that the contract the plaintiff describes is illegal and thus void or unenforceable as a matter of law.

In deciding a motion to dismiss, a court accepts the factual statements in the complaint as true,[8] and a defendant cannot introduce evidence outside the four corners of the complaint.[9] Thus, a defendant is limited in the arguments he can make. For example, in a contract case, a defendant could not argue that a plaintiff's allegation that the defendant offered him a job over the telephone was false. Instead, he could argue that the offer, as the plaintiff described it in the complaint, was not legally sufficient to form a contract.

If the defendant wins, the court may allow the plaintiff to amend the complaint. If the flaw in the complaint is one of insufficient facts, the court often will allow an amendment. However, if the claim is one that is so legally flawed that it can never succeed (such as the contract-for-murder example above), the court will likely dismiss the claim outright. If that claim is the only one in

---

5. *See, e.g.,* Foley v. Wells Fargo Bank, N.A., 772 F.3d 63, 72 (1st Cir. 2014).

6. Bell Atlantic Corp. v. Twombly, 550 U.S. 544, 556, 570 (2007).

7. Many scholars have argued that the heightened plausibility standard imposed in *Twombly, id.,* and *Ashcroft v. Iqbal,* 556 U.S. 662, 677–680 (2009), has achieved exactly that goal, and that plaintiffs with valid claims have been blocked from the courts. *See, e.g.,* Patricia W. Hatamyar, *The Tao of Pleading: Do Twombly and Iqbal Matter Empirically?,* 59 AM. U.L. REV. 553, 597–602 (2010) (finding that the percentage of Rule 12(b)(6) dismissals increased significantly following the *Iqbal* decision).

8. *Iqbal,* 556 U.S. at 678.

9. Usually, if the defendant does introduce evidence outside the complaint, the motion is transformed from one to dismiss to one for summary judgment. *See* FED. R. CIV. P. 12(d).

the case, then the court may enter a final judgment, after which the plaintiff can appeal. But if one claim is dismissed and others are not, the case usually continues to the next stage on those claims that remain.[10]

2. Motion for Summary Judgment

If a defendant chooses not to file a motion to dismiss, or if not all her claims are dismissed at the motion-to-dismiss stage, the defendant will file an answer to the complaint. The case then proceeds to the discovery stage, which involves uncovering the facts of the case. Discovery takes many forms: subpoenas, depositions, and interrogatories are a few of the most common. The strategic choices you make at this stage are exceedingly important and are discussed in more detail in Chapter 3.

Once discovery is complete—which can take months, sometimes years— either party can file a motion for summary judgment.[11] Under Rule 56 of the Federal Rules of Civil Procedure, a judge may grant this motion when there is no dispute of material fact and the moving party is entitled to judgment as a matter of law.[12]

A fatal error here is for the movant to present a factual story that conflicts with the non-movant's material facts. This is the boundary that you must not cross if you aim to win your motion for summary judgment.

The following example from a summary judgment brief avoids this pitfall by pointing to the plaintiffs' own words to show that the alleged oral agreement was too complicated and novel to be enforced without a written contract:

> Courts have long recognized that some agreements are so complex or so novel that as a matter of law they simply must be in writing in order to be enforced. This is such an agreement. It involved potentially tens of millions of dollars (Dubuc Decl. ¶3), was undisputedly "unprecedented" (Davis 3/8 Tr. 87:7) and by plaintiffs' own account could run for decades. Davis 3/8 Tr. 108:2-7, 293:23-295:5. A writing therefore

---

10. That said, per Rule 54(b) of the Federal Rules of Civil Procedure, a court may enter a final judgment as to fewer than all of the claims or parties if the court finds there is no just reason for delay.

11. Technically, the parties can file motions for summary judgment at any time until thirty days after the close of discovery. FED. R. CIV. P. 56(b).

12. FED. R. CIV. P. 56(a).

was legally necessary to bind the parties. *See Braun v. CMGI, Inc.*, 64 Fed. Appx. 301, 303 (2d Cir. 2003)....[13]

Notice how the brief does not argue that the plaintiff is lying, or that the plaintiff and defendant disagree about whether the alleged agreement was complicated. Instead, the brief points to the specific facts that show that the plaintiff *agrees* the agreement was complex and novel; it then argues that the defendant is entitled to judgment as a matter of law based on those specific facts.

Of course, the plaintiff in this case could point the judge to one of two things: (1) a dispute of material fact, or (2) a different legal conclusion based on the undisputed facts. Opposing counsel in the above case thus might argue something like this:

> This oral agreement was a simple one: a 50/50 split of the profits from the show "Flip This House." It required no written agreement because the terms were uncomplicated. In his deposition, Davis stated that the agreement "could not be simpler." Davis 3/8 Tr. 107:2-4. It thus does not need to be in writing in order to be enforced, as the defendants claim. At the very least, the relative complexity of the contract is a dispute of fact that must be resolved by the jury.

Notice how the plaintiff first reframes the contract as a simple 50/50 split. That description is not at odds with the defendant's claims that the contract could involve millions of dollars and last for decades, so it does not create an issue of material fact. But it does support a different legal conclusion: that the terms of the contract were so simple that no writing was required.

And the plaintiff has a fallback position. Even if his version of the story is not enough to prevail, then at the very least the defendant's motion should be denied because the complexity of the contract is a factual question for the jury to decide.

Thus, in summary-judgment-motion practice, the circle of possible arguments broadens from where it is at the motion-to-dismiss stage. But strict boundaries persist: If your aim is a grant of the motion for summary judgment, avoid any potential conflicts of material fact. And if your aim is a denial of the motion, identify the plethora of factual disputes that must be solved by the factfinder.

---

13. Memorandum in Support of Defendants' Motion for Summary Judgment at 20, Trademark Props. Inc. v. A&E Television Networks, No. 2:06-cv-02195-CWH (D.S.C. Apr. 13, 2007).

3. Trial & Verdict

Once the trial starts, fact-finding begins. The boundaries on arguments are weaker now, set mainly by the rules of evidence and standards of proof. While the many rules of evidence are far beyond the scope of this book, below is a brief overview of the two main standards of proof in a civil case: "preponderance of the evidence" or "clear and convincing evidence."[14]

A preponderance of the evidence standard is the lowest burden a party must shoulder, and it is the most common one in civil cases. To prevail under a preponderance standard, a plaintiff must provide evidence showing that his claim is more likely true than not true.[15] This low standard is the default for civil trials as what is at stake is often money as compensation for an injury; an individual's fundamental rights or freedoms are not on the line.[16]

The clear and convincing evidence standard is a higher burden of proof. When faced with this burden, a plaintiff must provide the factfinder with the firm belief or conviction that it is highly probable that the factual contentions of the claim are true.[17] This standard is generally reserved for cases where something more than money is at stake.

Each of these standards will mold the arguments that lawyers make to the factfinder, but they constrain the parties far less than the standards for pretrial motions do.

B. Appeal

Once a final judgment is entered, the losing party may appeal. And at the appellate court, too, boundaries are placed on arguments by the standards the court applies. At this level, the standards are referred to as the standards of re-

---

14. In a criminal trial, the prosecution must prove its case "beyond a reasonable doubt," the highest possible standard of proof.

15. *See, e.g.*, 32A C.J.S. *Evidence* § 1628 (Westlaw 2016) ("A preponderance of evidence means evidence that is of greater weight, or is more convincing, than that offered in opposition;....").

16. *See, e.g.*, Grogan v. Garner, 498 U.S. 279, 286 (1991) ("[W]e presume that this [preponderance] standard is applicable in civil actions between private litigants unless 'particularly important individual interests or rights are at stake.'" (internal citations omitted)).

17. *See* Colorado v. New Mexico, 467 U.S. 310, 316 (1984) (citing C. McCormick, Law of Evidence § 320).

view. The different standards refer to the level of deference the appellate court will give to the trial court.

In the federal system, and in most state systems, trial courts are the finders of fact, and appellate courts are the arbiters of law. Because their decisions are binding on lower courts, appellate courts have the power to clarify ambiguities in the law or craft new legal rules. Thus, the level of deference appellate courts give to trial courts' decisions depends on whether the question posed is one of law or one of fact. If it is one of law, the appellate courts grant almost no deference. If it is one of fact, the appellate courts substantially defer to the findings of the trial courts.

To find the standard of review, look first to past appellate cases that have decided the same issue. For example, you would know that an appeal of a motion for summary judgment receives *de novo* review because every federal appellate circuit has said so. But you also know that this is the correct standard because motions for summary judgment decide questions of law, not questions of fact. Rarely, novel legal issues may require an appellate court to determine the applicable standard of review; then, your argument as to which standard applies mainly will rest on whether the question is one of fact or law.

1. Standards of Review

De novo. This level of review is reserved for pure questions of law. You will commonly see it applied to reviews of grants of motions to dismiss or motions for summary judgment, where, typically, the question was a legal one. Under *de novo* review, appellate courts grant no deference to the court's decision below; the appellate court looks at the issue anew and decides the legal question for itself.

Clear error. This level of deference applies to questions of fact and is a higher hurdle to clear than the *de novo* standard. Under this standard, it is not enough that the appellate court would have decided the case differently if presented with the same set of facts. As the Supreme Court framed it: A finding is only clearly erroneous when "the reviewing court on the entire evidence is left with the definite and firm conviction that a mistake has been committed."[18] The appellate court is thus generally deferring to a trial court's decision and will only overturn that decision if it is clear the trial court made a mistake.

---

18. Anderson v. City of Bessemer, 470 U.S. 564, 573 (1985) (quoting *United States v. U.S. Gypsum Co.*, 333 U.S. 364, 395 (1948)).

What might satisfy this standard? One possibility is that the district court's conclusion is not supported by the evidence in the record. For example, one appellate court found clear error when a district court's decision was "unsupported by the record evidence and directly contradicted by the undisputed record and testimony by neutral parties...."[19] This finding was in a case where a prison supervisor testified that her motive for increasing a prisoner's security level was due to the fact that she believed him to be a security risk, but that testimony was contradicted by her own written statements at the time of the increase in security level, as well as the testimony of three other witnesses who stated that the supervisor had attempted to retaliate against the prisoner in the past.[20] That was enough for the court to overturn the district court's finding in favor of the supervisor, even under a clear error standard.[21]

On the other hand, it is not clear error when the evidence points to two plausible conclusions, and the district court chooses one conclusion over the other.[22] For example, in an employment discrimination case, multiple witnesses told varying version of events, and the district court found the evidence supporting the plaintiff's argument, including her testimony, to be credible.[23] That conclusion was not clear error because the finding was based on the judge's decision to credit the plaintiff's testimony, and that witness told "a coherent and facially plausible story that is not contradicted by extrinsic evidence...."[24]

Obviously, the line between clear error and no clear error is a fine and ambiguous one. As an advocate, the wisest course is to use the standard to your advantage. Highlight the standard when it favors you (e.g., when your opponent must overcome a clearly erroneous bar); mention but de-emphasize it when it harms you.

Abuse of Discretion. The highest level of deference given to a district court decision is an abuse of discretion standard. This standard of review depends not on the nature of the question posed (fact vs. law), but whether the decision is of a type that is traditionally reserved to the trial court's judgment.[25] Many decisions pertaining to supervision of litigation—such as the grant or denial of an objection, or the admission of documents into evidence—are

---

19. King v. Zamiara, 680 F.3d 686, 702 (6th Cir. 2012) (internal citation omitted).
20. *Id.* at 698–702.
21. *Id.* at 701–02.
22. *Anderson,* 470 U.S. at 574.
23. *See id.* at 567–571.
24. *Id.* at 575 (internal citations omitted).
25. Harry T. Edwards & Linda A. Elliot, Federal Courts Standards of Review 67 (2007).

committed to a judge's discretion because those questions often have more than one legally correct answer.[26] If a legal issue necessitates an abuse of discretion standard, the language of the statute or rule governing that issue will often expressly require it.

A judge abuses her discretion when she (1) fails to consider a factor relevant to the decision; (2) considers and gives significant weight to an irrelevant or improper factor; or (3) makes a clear error of judgment.[27] One example of abuse of discretion occurred when a judge failed to consider each of the factors Congress laid out for dismissing a criminal case with prejudice under the Speedy Trial Act.[28] In addition, the factors the trial court did rely on "were unsupported by factual findings or evidence in the record."[29]

Despite this fairly cogent example of abuse of discretion, the standard is a fuzzy one. As one scholar noted, "[T]here are at least weak and strong senses of 'discretion' and in reality 'abuse of discretion' may invoke a broad spectrum of review standards and applications."[30] The best advice here is to look to the precedents in the specific context of your case (e.g., a denial of a motion to stay, or the grant of an objection) to determine how past courts have applied this standard in that context.

---

26. *Id.*
27. *See* Kern v. TXO Prod. Corp., 738 F.2d 968, 970 (8th Cir. 1984).
28. United States v. Taylor, 487 U.S. 326, 327–32 (1988).
29. *Id.* at 343–44.
30. Steven Alan Childress, *Standards of Review Primer: Federal Civil Appeals*, 229 F.R.D. 267, 294 (2005) (internal citations omitted).

Chapter 3

The Role of Facts

Every case has a factual and legal component. Although you might assume that facts are the easy part, this chapter will introduce their less obvious qualities. As with law, facts must be found, selected, and used strategically.

Sometimes the facts are not in dispute. For example, in a pre-trial dispositive motion, a judge generally applies the law to the facts as stated in the complaint, which should be accepted as true, as discussed in Chapter 2. But at other stages of a litigation, opposing parties have competing versions of facts, and factfinders must decide which version to believe.

The capacity of facts to be true or false is, to an extent, their essential quality; the automobile was moving at 75 m.p.h. or it was not. Adjectives, by comparison, are inherently personal; their meaning varies across speakers. A speeding ticket requires more evidence than a witness stating "she was driving fast" because we have no guarantee that "fast" to Ivan is "fast" to Yann.

However, objective verifiability does not alone determine relevance in a legal dispute. Whether the car was a BMW or a Buick is a fact, but not one that is determinative of the legal outcome here, a potential speed limit violation. The make of the car might, however, be an important fact in a different legal context, for example if there were any question of manufacturer liability. In this respect, facts and law are mutually determinative: you cannot research the law without knowledge of the facts, but the law helps establish which facts are relevant.

Yet, a fact with no direct legal consequence is not necessarily an irrelevant fact. This is because decision-makers lack perfect knowledge and inevitably fill factual voids with inferences. And because decision-makers are human, these inferences will be shaped by personal morals, social values, experience, and human nature. If all legal disputes could be resolved by feeding a set of facts and a rule of law into an algorithm, we would not need appellate courts, or concurrences and dissents. There would be perfect consensus as to the right answer in every case.

Instead of using binary constructs like true versus false, think of facts as ingredients in a litigation recipe. Facts are most powerfully conveyed through narrative—not narratives that tug at the heartstrings, but narratives that unite fact and law.[1] Every litigation contains multiple narratives, many of which lawyers construct, reconstruct, and vary according to context, audience, procedural stage, learned facts, and substantive law, among other factors. Some of these retellings occur through formal court documents while others operate beyond the court's purview, in a "parallel procedural universe" that includes demand letters, memoranda, office email, correspondence with the client, notes, and drafts.[2]

A judicial opinion also contains a narrative—the official version of the facts that becomes precedent. Although it may impress readers as conveying a single, immutable set of facts, the final narrative is not necessarily the complete truth or the only possible truth. A legal dispute may be resolved even if some facts remain unknown. Perhaps the main witness has died or key evidence destroyed. Perhaps the case is dismissed for procedural reasons, such as for lack of jurisdiction or because the statute of limitations has run, in which case the critical conduct is never adjudicated. Some facts are discovered but deemed inadmissible at trial under the rules of evidence, never entering the competing narratives presented to the jury.

Moreover, even within the universe of known and admissible facts, the ones appearing in the written opinion have been selected and portrayed, a process likened to a kind of art.[3] When you read opinions, pay attention to how facts are presented—especially at the outset of the story. You will find that the opening selection of facts frequently provide cues as to the outcome of the case.[4] Given this connection, we might think of judges as not merely decision-makers,

---

1. Some scholars have challenged the distinction between law and fact. *See generally* Ronald J. Allen & Michael S. Pardo, *The Myth of the Law-Fact Distinction*, 97 Nw. U. L. Rev. 1769 (2003). The issue arises when fact assessments are embedded in rules, as will be discussed in the next chapter.

2. *See* Stephen N. Subrin & Thomas O. Main, *The Integration of Law and Fact in an Uncharted Parallel Universe*, 79 Notre Dame L. Rev. 1981, 1983–84 (2004).

3. *See* Stewart G. Pollock, *The Art of Judging*, 71 N.Y.U. L. Rev. 591, 594 (1996) ("[T]he art of judging begins with the portrayal of the facts.").

4. *See* Patricia M. Wald, *The Rhetoric of Results and the Results of Rhetoric: Judicial Writings*, 62 U. Chi. L. Rev. 1371, 1377 (1995) ("In virtually all cases, the judge shapes her raw material. She picks her rhetoric to foreshadow the result.").

but authors. And because appellate judges learn the facts from the attorneys' briefs, attorneys play a critical role in shaping these opinions.[5]

Later in the textbook we will discuss techniques for persuasively presenting facts, but our immediate focus is on the basic forms and reasons for which facts are collected, sorted, and processed prior to that point—and the considerations attendant to these choices. In practice, lawyers must critically evaluate the facts at almost every stage and often make decisions with incomplete knowledge of the facts. At all points, clients expect their lawyers to make efficient choices (i.e., only undertake those actions in which the benefit exceeds the cost), which requires strategic and thoughtful planning.

A. Gathering Facts

Sometimes all critical facts are easily acquired from the client at the outset, but often not. Which facts are relevant depends upon the substantive law, litigation stage, and strategy. The lawyer must decide what facts need to be known at each point, figure out how to obtain the facts, and determine at what point she has "enough" factual knowledge to take the next step (e.g., take on a new client, depose the head of a company, make a motion for summary judgment, settle the case, go to trial, etc.).

Lawyers select legally relevant facts from pools of varying sizes. Some problems are more fact-specific than others. Resolving a simple breach of contract action between two parties may require little more than examining the language used in the contract and the conduct allegedly causing its breach. On the other hand, modern complex commercial litigations usually involve multiple parties and multiple claims, often applying novel legal theories to a vast network of fact scenarios and divergent narratives. In such a situation, even the starting point for fact-gathering may be non-obvious.

Some standard methods for collecting information about a problem, initially and at later stages, are introduced below.

1. Client Interview

Although you may interact with a client throughout a litigation, a lawyer often must decide at the outset whether to take on a case or make a prediction about its likely outcome. In addition to reviewing any immediately-available

---

5. There is ample literature devoted to lawyering and storytelling. *See generally, e.g.,* PHILIP N. MEYER, STORYTELLING FOR LAWYERS (2014).

documentary or other evidence, collecting an initial set of facts involves interviewing a prospective client.

As a method of gathering relevant facts, a client interview can be like trying to catch a fish with your hands. Events considered important to the client may have little or no relevance to what the law considers important. Further, people do not tend to speak in an organized and complete manner. For these reasons, lawyers must ask follow-up questions, aimed at eliciting facts untold and perhaps not recalled. To ask effective follow-up questions, the lawyer needs a good sense of the relevant law. This recursive process of ascertaining the relevant law and relevant facts is a hallmark of preparing a legal analysis.

Even when responding to focused questioning, a client's recounting of an emotionally-charged experience is like anyone's: subjective. Favorable facts may be inadvertently enhanced in the retelling and details contravening the client's emotional experience neglected. Advances in neuroscience have revealed the brain's ability to filter, embellish, and rewrite experience through memory,[6] an inescapable assault on objective facts to which the legal system is susceptible at various stages, despite formal precautions.[7] And potential clients may withhold some relevant details unwittingly in the process of concealing other information, unrelated to the litigation, yet possibly unflattering, embarrassing, or illegal. Clients want to be seen in the best light, including by their attorney.

Even once you achieve proficiency in eliciting relevant facts, whether an interview provides sufficient information to move forward with a case varies. The next section addresses how additional facts may be learned from your client's adversary after the litigation has been formally initiated.

2. Discovery

Discovery refers to the formal procedure by which each party obtains evidence from the other side. There are different forms of discovery, but the most common include:

- Depositions. Depositions involve one party's lawyers questioning witnesses associated with the adversary, demanded by serving a

---

6. *See* Daniel Kahneman, THINKING FAST AND SLOW 377–81 (2011).

7. *See generally* Aileen P. Clare, *Is Eyewitness Testimony Inherently Unreliable?*, ABA SECTION OF LITIGATION (May 28, 2012), http://apps.americanbar.org/litigation/committees/trialevidence/articles/winterspring2012-0512-eyewitness-testimony-unreliable.html; Henry F. Fradella, *Why Judges Should Admit Expert Testimony on the Unreliability of Eyewitness Testimony*, 2 FED. CTS. L. REV. 1 (2007); *see also* Francis X. Shen, *The Law and Neuroscience Bibliography: Navigating the Emerging Field of Neurolaw*, 38 INT'L J. LEGIS. INFO. 352 (2010).

subpoena. The assumption is that witnesses associated with each party offer statements voluntarily, whereas those associated with the adversary must be legally compelled. Depositions are taken under oath and can be lengthy; the questioning attorney is attempting to find critical information, often without knowledge of exactly what that information is, from a witness disinclined to divulge anything. Depositions are recorded and can be offered as evidence.

- Document Production. A party may request that the opposing party provide potentially relevant documents, usually by category (e.g., all correspondence between X and Y transmitted during the period from May 2, 2009 to August 15, 2012).
- Interrogatories. Interrogatories give the parties an opportunity to demand answers to questions. The questions may be specific but are often aimed at acquiring a lot of information in hopes that something relevant will emerge.

Although you might assume that sweeping discovery should be conducted in all situations to increase the likelihood of obtaining "the truth," other considerations make this strategy much more selective. For example, if you are fairly certain that the plaintiff's claim can be dismissed by a motion to dismiss, you might not engage in any discovery. If the motion is successful, you will have successfully represented the client for the lowest possible cost. Most decisions about pursuing facts and other matters of strategy implicate this type of cost-benefit analysis.[8]

B. Selecting and Communicating Facts in Writing

The facts you select to include in any given writing, and their presentation, will be influenced by many factors, including the purpose of and audience for the document, the relevant law, and the procedural posture.

To get started thinking about facts in ways that will productively influence your choices, consider some fundamental categories of facts in the context of a legal analysis.

---

8. In practice, you may hear reference to discovery requests as "fishing expeditions," a derogatory phrase used when one side believes the other has no evidence or sound theory that the law has been violated and thus makes sweeping requests for information in hopes of uncovering something.

- Legally determinative or "material": these facts are essential to the outcome of the case; in their absence, the result would differ. Determinative facts must be considered, regardless of whether they help or harm your client.
- Relevant, but not necessarily outcome-determinative: some facts do not make or break the outcome but still play an important role. They may, for example, be helpful in conveying a coherent narrative, providing context for understanding the more relevant act. Some facts help introduce a sympathetic aspect of your client—but avoid confusing these facts with adjectives and adverbs that merely induce skepticism in readers.
- Red herrings: these facts seem like they should be relevant, but actually relate to an irrelevant point of law or emotional trigger.
- Irrelevant: these facts should be avoided. Although identifying irrelevant facts sounds self-evident, these facts are often ones that new lawyers lean toward including simply because of their certainty. But including too many concrete facts, like unnecessary dates, can obscure more important facts.
- Not facts: the "not facts" category includes adjectives and adverbs, along with legal conclusions or inferences. These should generally be avoided in your fact descriptions, if possible, as they are disputable and thus can have the effect of weakening your narrative.

The proper category of a given fact may not be obvious at first. Litigations are dynamic creatures, resetting the relevant facts at different points in time—a judge may dispose of one claim but allow another to move forward; your adversary may move for summary judgment; some facts may be relevant to negotiating a settlement yet not necessary for the present procedural stage.

Eventually, you will also discover that classifying facts is as much a product of legal argument as of any objective qualities. Legal argument includes persuading the court of the relative legal significance (or insignificance) of a particular fact, e.g., your adversary's purportedly determinative fact is, you would try to demonstrate, a red herring.

Keep in mind that the most credible, compelling narratives are substantially comprised of relevant, undeniably true facts. When you communicate the facts in any legal writing, get in the habit of sifting out adjectives, adverbs, subjective characterizations, and legal conclusions.

Compare the following two descriptions and ask yourself which one is more easily disputed by the defendant:

- The defendant acted in an extremely threatening manner, insinuating his ability to use a weapon.
- The defendant opened his jacket to reveal a gun.

The first assertion would be open to any number of unverifiable refutations (His conduct was not extremely threatening. His conduct did not attempt to insinuate.). The second sentence doesn't blink.

Chapter 4

Legal Rules

In law, rules are everywhere. Some are explicitly stated in statutes and regulations. Others are implicitly contained in court opinions. Some are binding, others persuasive. Some rules even conflict with one another. In many ways, the practice of law is, at its core, understanding and using rules. This chapter provides a foundation for developing those skills, with emphasis on statutory interpretation and synthesizing rules from case law.

A. Introduction to Rules

For present purposes, think of rules as generalized statements that prescribe lawful conduct, by permitting, prohibiting, or requiring some type of action.[1] This section addresses where to find rules, the forms they take, and basic policy implications.

1. Sources of Rules

Rules arise from different sources. Statutes are prototypical rules because they are generalized or abstract, enacted by legislatures to govern prospectively. Cases are particularized stories, inspired by circumstances that have already happened. But a well-written opinion will apply a generalized rule to the facts to reach its holding. Through this process, discussed in more detail in Part C of this chapter, common law rules arise.

---

1. *See* STEPHEN J. BURTON, AN INTRODUCTION TO LAW AND LEGAL REASONING 13–14 (3d ed. 2007). Unlike rules of science, which are verifiable, rules of law are prescriptive — they are about regulating conduct and problem solving. *See id.* at 82–85.

Some common law rules are neatly packaged by your jurisdiction's high court. For example, the Supreme Court of Oklahoma created four different rules in one case, stating, "[b]y our decision today, we ... recognize the tort of invasion of privacy in all four categories as set out in the Restatement."[2] The rules articulated by that court, even if adopted from a secondary source, subsequently bound lower courts.[3]

Although common law rules often arise in places where statutes have not spoken, in our highly codified world, court-made rules also frequently appear as interpretive aides to statutory text.[4] That is, courts articulate rules that help apply the statutory rule to particular circumstances. For example, a California statute penalizes a person who "falsely personates another" for purposes of obtaining a benefit.[5] In a decision applying that rule, the California Supreme Court had to decide whether "another" included a dead person (and held that it did).[6] Lower courts applying that statute are thereafter bound by the California Supreme Court's holding—even though the statutory text never explains who may qualify as "another."

The interpretive rule to be drawn from that case is explicit: "another" includes the dead. But the more challenging situation is finding a rule in a vaguely-worded judicial opinion. How can a rule be applied when it is never articulated? In this situation, we borrow the advice of Orin Kerr: embrace the ambiguity.[7] Do not distort the law by reducing it to a simplistic certainty but accept that law is sometimes unclear.[8] As the next section illustrates, ambiguity is a common attribute of rules. Learning to use it effectively is a valued skill in lawyering.

2. Types of Rules

Rules come in different shapes and sizes. Sometimes they are organized around a single criterion, like a statute of limitations requiring that an action

---

2. McCormack v. Oklahoma Publ'g Co., 613 P.2d 737, 740 (Okla. 1980).

3. *See id.* at 740–42 (quoting the Restatement of Torts in recognizing the tort of invasion of privacy).

4. Judith S. Kaye, *State Courts at the Dawn of a New Century: Common Law Courts Reading Statutes and Constitutions*, 70 N.Y.U.L. Rev. 1, 8 (1995) ("[D]espite the continued vitality of the common law, it is clear that 'common law judging' now takes place in a 'world of statutes.'" (citing Ellen A. Peters, *Common Law Judging in a Statutory World: An Address*, 43 U. Pitt. L. Rev. 995, 995–96 (1982)).

5. *See* Cal. Penal Code § 529 (West).

6. *See* Lee v. Superior Court, 989 P.2d 1277, 1278–79, 1280 (Cal. 2000).

7. *See* Orin S. Kerr, *How to Read a Legal Opinion: A Guide for New Law Students*, 11 Green Bag 2d 51, 60 (2007).

8. *Id.* at 60–61.

must be brought within one year of its accrual. But often a rule has more than one component, in which case the attorney must initially determine what its components are and how they interrelate. Here are some fundamental types of rule components.

Elements. The "elements" of a rule are its required conditions: what *must* happen to trigger the remedy, privilege, or penalty associated with the rule. When faced with this type of rule, your first step is to break it down into a list of its elements.

Say your client seeks advice about legal recourse against a co-worker who spread untrue rumors about her. Under the relevant common law rule, "[t]o establish a claim for defamation, a plaintiff must show that a defendant made a defamatory statement about the plaintiff and published the statement to a third party."[9] This rule has two elements: (1) a defamatory statement; and (2) publication to a third party. Neither one alone supports a legal action. Together, they do (the elements may be described as "conjunctive").

Now consider a statutory rule aimed at protecting a person's "right of publicity":

> A person, firm or corporation that uses for advertising purposes, or for the purposes of trade, the name, portrait or picture of any living person without having first obtained the written consent of such person, or if a minor of his or her parent or guardian, is guilty of a misdemeanor.[10]

By separating and enumerating the elements, you can more easily assess whether the client's facts can meet each one.

1. A person, firm or corporation
2. That uses for advertising purposes or for the purposes of trade
3. The name, portrait or picture
4. Of a living person
5. Without prior written consent

The order in which you list the elements matters less at this initial stage than understanding what they are and how they relate to one another. As this example illustrates, an element may offer several acceptable means of satisfaction (alternative requirements are referred to as "disjunctive"). Element 3 may be satisfied by the use of a name, portrait or picture. Under Element 2, it can be used for either advertising or trade purposes. If you separated these alternatives out into different elements, each of which needed to be satisfied,

---

9. Neumann v. Liles, 369 P.3d 1117, 1121 (Or. 2016) (internal citation omitted).
10. N.Y. Civ. Rights Law § 50 (McKinney).

you would misstate what the rule actually requires, and your analysis would be off-track from the start.

The break points of a rule may not be obvious from the language, so check whether any cases have already listed the elements. Cases may illuminate whether, for example, the phrase "breaking and entering" or "aiding and abetting" refers to two separate conditions or one. Case law can also clarify confusing modifiers like adjectives or adverbs. For example, assume the rule said "knowingly transfers, possesses, or uses the identification of another person." Does "knowingly" then modify only "transfers"? Or does it also modify "possesses" or "uses"? What about the "identification of another person" element; must the defendant also know that the ID belonged to another rather than being a counterfeit? These are questions courts struggle with, and referring to precedents can help you make sense of the muddle.[11]

Remember that an elements test means no partial credit: three out of four amounts to zero. The corollary to a plaintiff needing to establish all elements of a rule is that the defendant need merely defeat one element to win. It is not unusual for a dispute to turn on a single element. Whichever side you represent, learning all the elements at the outset is essential for an accurate assessment of the facts.

Some rules incorporate an exception, a specific condition that nullifies the rule's applicability or one of its requirements, like in the following example from the Uniform Commercial Code: "Words control figures except that if the words are ambiguous figures control."[12] An exception can be incorporated into an elements test, such that all the elements may be met, but if the facts of the case fall within the exception, then the remedy, privilege, or penalty is not triggered. A rule containing an exception, or list of exceptions, is also known as a "defeasible rule."[13]

Factors. Some rules are not elements tests, but instead are made up of factors that a court should consider in reaching its decision. For example, the Copyright Act provides for the "fair use" of a copyrighted work, assessed by recourse to four nonexclusive factors:

(1) the purpose and character of the use, including whether such use is of a commercial nature or is for nonprofit educational purposes;

---

11. *See, e.g.,* Flores-Figueroa v. United States, 556 U.S. 646, 650, 657 (2009) (finding "knowingly" to modify "identification of another person").

12. N.Y. U.C.C. Law § 3-118(c) (McKinney).

13. Whether defeasible rules are actually rules has been a source of theoretical debate. For an influential defense, see H.L.A. Hart, The Concept of Law 136 (1961) (asserting that a rule ending with an "unless" clause "is still a rule").

(2) the nature of the copyrighted work;

(3) the amount and substantiality of the portion used in relation to the copyrighted work as a whole; and

(4) the effect of the use upon the potential market for or value of the copyrighted work.[14]

These factors offer a spectrum of considerations, so that using a copyrighted work for commercial purposes (factor (1)) might still be a fair use if only a trivial portion of the work was used and it had a negligible effect on the market for the work (factors (3) and (4), respectively). Notice, also, that a factor may demand assessment of a characteristic or quality like "the nature of the copyrighted work," rather than satisfaction of a measurable act or condition. An example of the latter appears in the earlier-referenced right of publicity statute, where one of the elements simply requires no "prior written consent" for the relevant conduct.

Factors tests are often crafted by courts to guide the interpretation of broad language in enacted law or constitutional language.[15] For example, when applying the Fourth Amendment's broad protection of the home against "unreasonable searches and seizures,"[16] the U.S. Supreme Court established four factors that "influence" the extent to which the surrounding area is included: (1) the nature of the uses to which the area is put, (2) the steps taken by the resident to protect the area from observation, (3) the existence of a surrounding enclosure, and (4) the area's proximity to the home.[17]

Your initial approach to applying a factors test should mirror that of elements: break the rule down and list the relevant factors. The difference will be that even if the evidence tips against your client on one factor, the action may still be successful. In the parlance of courts, "no single factor is dispositive."[18] For this reason, the factors should not only be analyzed individually (like with elements), but also weighed in the aggregate to reach the ultimate conclusion.

Totality of the Circumstances. A rule that instructs courts to consider the totality of the circumstances is the most open-ended and fact-specific type.

---

14. 17 U.S.C. § 107.

15. *See, e.g.,* United States v. Deleon, 710 F.2d 1218, 1220 (7th Cir. 1983) ("The Supreme Court has established a four-part balancing test to determine whether a defendant's constitutional right to a speedy trial has been violated." (internal citation omitted)).

16. U.S. Const. amend. IV.

17. United States v. Dunn, 480 U.S. 294, 301 (1987).

18. CAE, Inc. v. Clean Air Eng'g, Inc., 267 F.3d 660, 678 (7th Cir. 2001) (internal citation omitted).

It is thus the most un-rule-like, since fact-finding is normally the province of the jury.[19]

Consider a provision in the Bankruptcy Code, allowing courts to discharge a person's debt in the absence of the requisite records if "such act or failure to act was justified under all of the circumstances of the case."[20] What can a court consider in deciding whether to excuse a debtor for lacking records? Anything.

Rules resting upon a determination of what is "reasonable" similarly open the field of inquiry, as made explicit in this rule: "Whether a time for taking an action required by the Uniform Commercial Code is reasonable depends on the nature, purpose and circumstances of the action."[21] Even when the rule does not specifically direct the decisionmaker to consider all of the circumstances, fact-specific breadth may be invited by the rule's terminology, like a rule extending time to commence an action when such an extension would serve "the interest of justice."[22]

Totality of the circumstances tests, or rules couched in discretionary terms, will be more difficult for an attorney to deconstruct at the front end than rules providing elements or menus of factors. In these situations, the attorney must mold the rule into more concrete form—not by relying exclusively on one's own personal beliefs but by researching authorities, like case law that has applied the rule previously. For example, a case applying New York's rule on extending time to file an action offers some specific guidance:

> [T]he court may consider diligence, or lack thereof, along with any other relevant factor in making its determination, including expiration of the Statute of Limitations, the meritorious nature of the cause of action, the length of delay in service, the promptness of a plaintiff's request for the extension of time, and prejudice to defendant.[23]

By identifying precedents that have applied the rule in the past, the attorney culls a list of factors by which to reliably assess a client's circumstances.

Many rules are hybrids of the types discussed above. You may have noticed that the New York rule quoted above provides specific factors, yet still remains

---

19. *See* Antonin Scalia, *The Rule of Law as a Law of Rules*, 56 U. Chi. L. Rev. 1175, 1180–81 (1989) (stating that when a judge applies a totality of the circumstances test, "he is not so much pronouncing the law in the normal sense as engaging in the less exalted function of fact finding").

20. 11 U.S.C. §727.

21. N.M. Stat. Ann. §55-1-205.

22. N.Y. C.P.L.R. §306-b (McKinney).

23. Leader v. Maroney, Ponzini & Spencer, 97 N.Y.2d 95, 105–06 (N.Y. 2001).

open-ended. Non-exclusive factor tests are common.[24] Or, a single element within a rule might be assessed through a balancing test.[25] Courts might assign varying weights to certain factors.[26] It is exactly because rules are slippery that your first step should be breaking them down into their component parts. Your second step should be researching how cases have applied the rule.

3. Bright Lines and Flexibility

As we have seen, rules can be rigid and category-driven (like speed limits) or flexible and fact-specific (like reasonableness tests). Let's briefly consider the policies underlying these two species of rules, which are usually discussed as rules and standards[27] (though for our purposes, standards are also rules).

Generically speaking, a legal system built upon rules reflects certain social values, such as a preference for order, consistency, and predictability over ad hoc and discretionary decisionmaking. However, the generalized fairness of bright-line rules can also compromise fair results in particular circumstances. We all know that the point of traffic lights is safety, but if a rule requires drivers to stop on red, then drivers must stop on red regardless of immediate conditions, e.g., clear weather, no cars or pedestrians in sight, a perfect driving record. One presupposition of a system of rules, Frederick Schauer has observed, is a willingness to enforce them even when the decisionmaker dislikes the outcome (or dislikes the rule).[28]

However, as discussed, the degree to which a rule dictates an outcome varies, revealing preferences about who should be entrusted with power and how it should be allocated.[29] At one end are simple, objective categories, like age-

---

24. *See, e.g., Dunn*, 480 U.S. at 301 (noting that the factors should not be applied formulaically but in light of the totality of the circumstances).

25. *See, e.g., CAE, Inc.*, 267 F.3d at 677–78 (applying seven-factor balancing test to interpret element of a Lanham Act claim under 22 U.S.C. § 1125).

26. *See, e.g., id.* at 678.

27. *See generally, e.g.*, Frederick Schauer, *The Tyranny of Choice and the Rulification of Standards*, 14 J. Contemp. Legal Issues 803 (2005); Louis Kaplow, *Rules Versus Standards: An Economic Analysis*, 42 Duke L.J. 557 (1992); Pierre J. Schlag, *Rules and Standards*, 33 UCLA L. Rev. 379 (1985); *see also* Susan C. Morse, *Safe Harbors, Sure Shipwrecks*, 49 U.C. Davis L. Rev. 1385 (2016) (theorizing choices and incentives in legal regimes driven by hybrid forms of rules and standards).

28. *See* Frederick Schauer, Thinking Like a Lawyer: A New Introduction to Legal Reasoning 28, 35 (2009).

29. *See* Frederick Schauer, Playing by the Rules: A Philosophical Examination of Rule-Based Decision-Making in Law and in Life 173 (1991).

based rights (e.g., voting, driving, leasing). These rules yield consistent, predictable outcomes, reduce the potential for judicial bias, and promote administrative efficiency. Inhabitants of a jurisdiction that makes sixteen the minimum age to apply for a driver's license can organize their conduct with *ex ante* certainty of the legal outcome. The tradeoff is the imperfect correlation of such rules with equitable results in particular situations (you likely know many careless drivers over the age of sixteen).

Open-ended rules (standards), on the other hand, enable courts to address fairness for each set of facts. If the jurisdiction above replaced minimum age with the "ability to minimize risks," a skilled, careful fifteen-year-old might justifiably obtain a driver's license. But outcomes would become less predictable, with each decision funneled through a decisionmaker's personal values and experience. How would a person seeking a license plan when to apply or how to prepare?[30] Delays would proliferate and administrative costs would swell.[31]

But discretion and inefficiency in one context is sound policy in another. Rule 402 of the Federal Rules of Evidence, for example, invites situation-specific discretion by broadly stating that "relevant evidence is admissible."[32] The term "relevant" gives trial judges a degree of flexibility in individual cases (subject to specified constraints).[33] This makes sense, given the uniqueness of every case.

Discretionary rules are not necessarily aimed at enhancing the judicial role. They offer society at large a footpath to the courthouse, like the social norms summoned by tort law's "reasonable person." Rules contingent on "reasonableness" ensure ongoing dialogue with society. Further, some rules are open-textured yet tailored to a category of conduct, as when the Uniform Commercial Code renders an offer accepted "in any manner and by any medium reasonable in the circumstances."[34] The language sounds murky, but it draws from shared

---

30. The inability to organize conduct in light of foreseeable outcomes has been a critique of fairness-based decision-making in private law. *Cf., e.g.,* Frank H. Easterbrook, *Foreword: The Court and the Economic System*, 98 Harv. L. Rev. 4, 11–12 (1984) (arguing that the *ex post* nature of outcomes governed by flexible standards prevents parties from bargaining with full knowledge of their respective rights).

31. *See* Carol M. Rose, *Crystals and Mud in Property Law*, 40 Stan. L. Rev. 577, 609 (1988) (describing inefficiency as chief concern of those who prefer rules to standards).

32. Fed. R. Evid. 402 (subject to certain exceptions).

33. *E.g.,* United States v. Russell, 703 F.2d 1243, 1249 (11th Cir. 1983) (stating that "[d]eterminations of admissibility of evidence rest largely within the discretion of the trial judge...." (internal citations omitted)).

34. N.Y. U.C.C. Law §2-206 (McKinney).

business practices.[35] The Copyright Act leaves the door open for technological development by defining "copies" to include objects "in which a work is fixed by any method now known or later developed."[36]

Ultimately, the language of rules provides for endless combinations, degrees, mutability, and breadth. The above examples are better understood as points on a spectrum rather than mutually-exclusive boxes, and they only scratch the surface of how rules operate.

B. Statutory Interpretation: Language and Meaning

The main difference between a statutory rule and a rule derived from case law is the weight placed on the specific language of the rule. The words of a statute matter, inordinately. Why is this so? Because the language used in the statute was passed by a legislature; a court's task is only to interpret those words, to figure out what they mean when applied to a set of facts.

Rules derived from judicial opinions are less beholden to language. The same rule may be stated by a number of different judges using a variety of different words, each of which is acceptable. These variations in the rule from case to case may reflect the work of good lawyering. That process, called rule synthesis, is discussed in more detail at the end of this chapter.

In statutory interpretation, the focus of this section, the lawyer is restrained by the words on the page. The specific text offers the only authoritative version of the rule.[37] Although meaning is bounded by text, the elasticity between the two is what triggers the need for judicial interpretation.

1. Plain and Not Plain Meaning

First and foremost, any interpreter of statutes must attempt to find the words' "plain meaning." When the words are clear and unambiguous, courts

---

35. *See* Rose, *supra* note 31, at 609 (arguing that standards like "commercial reasonableness" in the U.C.C. offer greater predictability to business people than well-delineated abstractions).

36. 17 U.S.C. § 101.

37. *See* Paul T. Wangerin, *Skills Training in "Legal Analysis": A Systematic Approach*, 40 U. Miami L. Rev. 409, 438–39 (1986) (citing Harry W. Jones, *Notes on the Teaching of Legal Method*, 1 J. Legal Educ. 13, 23 (1948)).

look no further; they simply apply the rule to the facts.[38] If you run a red light, you have violated a traffic rule. There is no room to argue that the color red in a traffic light means anything other than "stop." Similarly, a rule prohibiting vehicles from entering a public park would stop a car carrying a family on its way to a picnic from entering the park. The plain meaning of the term "vehicles," most would agree, unambiguously encompasses automobiles.

Yet these unambiguous examples rarely cross the courthouse door. Rather, litigations are borne of plausible uncertainty. For example, assume that a statute prohibits "motorcycles" in a park. Does the plain meaning of that term also includes three-wheeled off-road vehicles? Reasonable minds could disagree.

In law, these uncertainties are not purely linguistic. Rather, questions of meaning may also arise when the meaning of the text is plain, but the result seems incongruous with the rule's function. For example, the "no vehicles in the park" rule, as noted above, easily embraces an automobile. But what if a veterans' organization wants to donate a functional military truck to serve as a war memorial, mounted on a pedestal for display purposes?

In the abstract, a truck is as much a vehicle as an automobile, but the result of that hypothetical seems unreasonable. Why? Because "vehicles," in the context of the rule, speaks to concerns regarding traffic flow and some related consequence, like safety or noise. A military truck used as a monument would only enter the park once and then remain motionless and silent. In other words, we normally would not categorize monuments and automobiles together for purposes of regulating traffic. Which meaning prevails under these circumstances? How do courts decide?

2. Theories of Statutory Interpretation

The "no vehicles in the park" hypothetical was the subject of a famous jurisprudential debate between H.L.A. Hart and Lon Fuller in 1958, and illustrates two central theories of statutory interpretation: textualism and purposivism. Hart used the "no vehicles in the park" example as support for his idea that statutory terms have a "core of settled meaning" that can be applied without

---

38. *See, e.g.*, King v. Burwell, 135 S. Ct. 2480, 2489 (2015) ("If the statutory language is plain, we must enforce it according to its terms." (internal citations omitted)); Caminetti v. United States, 242 U.S. 470, 485 (1917) ("Where the language is plain and admits of no more than one meaning, the duty of interpretation does not arise, and the rules which are to aid doubtful meanings need no discussion." (internal citation omitted)).

question; thus, "vehicle" would include an automobile.[39] The harder cases involve facts around the edges or "penumbra" (like a vehicle-monument), which require judicial decision.[40] Fuller, on the other hand, argued that the language of a rule has no "core meaning" independent of a statute's purpose.[41] Even applying the statute to an automobile requires some consideration of the statute's underlying purpose.[42]

Adhering to the literal meaning of words is known as "textualism." Applying textualist reasoning, the standard dictionary definition of "vehicle" would be determinative; thus, the military truck cannot enter the park. Deferring to a statute's purpose, sometimes even in contradiction of literal meaning, is called "purposivism." In a purposivist analysis, the "no vehicles" rule cannot reasonably be interpreted to ban monuments from parks, so the military truck may enter. These broadly-outlined interpretive theories remain integral to construing statutes today, and you may even encounter the "no vehicles in the park" hypothetical in discussions of statutory interpretation.[43]

Ultimately, both purposivism and textualism offer paths to determining meaning which, in an absolute sense, cannot be determined. Strict textualism prizes statutory language as the only legitimate source of meaning because of its seeming objectivity and as the most reliable expression of the enacting legislature's intent.[44] Congress selected and voted upon these particular

---

39. H.L.A. Hart, *Positivism and the Separation of Law and Morals*, 71 HARV. L. REV. 593, 607 (1958).

40. *Id.* The outlier nature of appellate decisions, as aberrations from the broader realm of legal disputes creates what is known as the "selection effect." *See, e.g.*, SCHAUER, *supra* note 28, at 22–23. George L. Priest & Benjamin Klein, *The Selection of Disputes for Litigation*, 13 J. LEGAL STUD. 1, 3–4 (1984).

41. Lon L. Fuller, *Positivism and Fidelity to Law—A Reply to Professor Hart*, 71 HARV. L. REV. 630, 663 (1958).

42. *Id.*

43. *E.g.*, F.C.C. v. NextWave Pers. Commc'ns Inc., 537 U.S. 293, 311 (2003) (Breyer, J., dissenting) ("'No vehicles in the park' does not refer to baby strollers or even to tanks used as part of a war memorial." (internal citation omitted)); Dep't of Commerce v. U.S. House of Representatives, 525 U.S. 316, 350 (1999) ("The 'except' clause does not necessarily apply to every conceivable use of statistical sampling any more than, say, a statutory rule forbidding 'vehicles' in the park applies to everything that could possibly be characterized as a 'vehicle.'" (internal citation omitted)); *see generally* Frederick Schauer, *A Critical Guide to Vehicles in the Park*, 83 N.Y.U. L. REV. 1109 (2008).

44. *See, e.g.*, People v. Hanna, 207 Ill. 2d 486, 497–98 (2003) ("The most reliable indicator of legislative intent is found in the language of the statute itself ... and that language should be given its plain, ordinary and popularly understood meaning...." (internal citations omitted)).

words, the reasoning goes, so courts must apply those words as a matter of legislative supremacy.[45] But the presumption of a monolithic intent shared by all voting members of a legislative body is a fictional construct. Thus, textualism can be seen more as a mechanism of enforcing judicial restraint than a quest for "true" meaning.[46]

Purposivism loosens the shackles of literalism but likewise seeks objectivity via the democratic system of legislative supremacy. Purposivist theory emphasizes that all rules are enacted to serve a purpose, and deference to statutory purpose best carries out the legislature's intent where language is ambiguous. This approach affords the judiciary some leeway in filling unavoidable gaps, like a legislature's inability to predict future scenarios or the inherent vagaries of language, while remaining faithful to the rule's animating purpose over mere form. Of course, this theory also rests on a similar fiction of legislative process, like a reasoned, unitary purpose among legislators, devoid of political compromise or competing influences.

At the extreme end of purposive reasoning lies a unique category of cases in which a court deviates from unambiguous language in the name of avoiding unjust, unreasonable, or absurd results—sometimes called the "absurdity doctrine." This theory postulates that legislative intent includes delegating some authority to courts to make corrections, as necessary.[47]

Which theory will reign in a given Supreme Court case is often unpredictable. In *United States v. Locke*, the Supreme Court adhered to literal meaning despite an apparent instance of careless legislative drafting.[48] The statute at issue required owners of mining property in Nevada to renew their mining claims "prior to December 31" of any given year.[49] Because the phrase "prior to December 31" literally means by December 30, the petitioners' claims

---

45. *See, e.g.*, United States v. Locke, 471 U.S. 84, 95 (1985) (reasoning that "deference to the supremacy of the Legislature, as well as recognition that Congressmen typically vote on the language of a bill, generally requires us to assume that 'the legislative purpose is expressed by the ordinary meaning of the words used'") (internal citation omitted).

46. *See* Victoria F. Nourse, *A Decision Theory of Statutory Interpretation: Legislative History by the Rules*, 122 YALE L. J. 70, 76 (2012) (describing intent as "a constitutional heuristic" aimed at restraining judges).

47. *See, e.g.*, United States v. Kirby, 74 U.S. 482, 486–87 (1868) ("It will always, therefore, be presumed that the legislature intended exceptions to its language, which would avoid [injustice, oppression, or absurd results]."); Sorrells v. United States, 287 U.S. 435, 448 (1932) ("We are not forced by the letter to do violence to the spirit and purpose of the statute."); Church of the Holy Trinity v. United States, 143 U.S. 457, 460 (1892).

48. 471 U.S. 84, 95–96 (1985).

49. *Id.* at 93.

were filed one day late, rendering their highly lucrative property claims abandoned and void.[50] The petitioners argued they had complied with the statute's purpose by filing before the end of the calendar year, which was certainly what the legislature had intended—but to no avail.[51] The plain language governed.[52]

On the other hand, in *Bond v. United States*,[53] the Supreme Court yielded to legislative assumptions that "go without saying."[54] In *Bond*, a microbiologist learned that her husband had fathered a child with her best friend; she then placed toxic chemicals on the ex-friend's door knob, mailbox, and car, intending to cause a rash.[55] Her actions resulted in a minor chemical burn on the victim's thumb, treated by rinsing with water.[56] Defendant Bond was charged with violating the federal Chemical Weapons Convention Implementation Act, enacted pursuant to an international treaty aimed at eliminating weapons of mass destruction, including chemical warfare.[57]

Although the plain language of the statute covered Bond's use of the chemical, the Court reversed her conviction. Interpreting statutory language, the majority stated, requires recognizing that "'Congress legislates against the backdrop' of certain unexpressed presumptions."[58] Here, the operative presumption was a state's sovereignty in penalizing local crimes; had Congress intended to interfere with this balance between state and federal criminal jurisdiction, the Court reasoned, it would have done so explicitly in the text.[59] Justice Scalia dissented with his characteristic textualist stance, asserting, "Today, the Court shirks its job and performs Congress's."[60]

Ultimately, the theoretical underpinnings of interpreting statutes support a wide variety of approaches, some overlapping, others conflicting, and all eluding a single decisive path to meaning.[61] The next section offers a more

---

50. *Id.* at 89–91.

51. *Id.* at 93–94.

52. *Id.*

53. 134 S. Ct. 2077 (2014).

54. *Id.* at 2088.

55. *Id.* at 2085.

56. *Id.*

57. *Id.*

58. *Id.* (internal citation omitted).

59. *Id.* at 2089–90.

60. *Id.* at 2094 (Scalia, J., dissenting).

61. *See generally* William N. Eskridge, Jr. & Philip P. Frickey, *Statutory Interpretation as Practical Reasoning*, 42 STAN. L. REV. 321 (1990) (arguing that each major theory, intentionalism, purposivism, and textualism, is ultimately indeterminate and cannot be wholly severed from the other theories).

pragmatic toolbox for clearing the brush and forging a path appropriate to each case.

3. Tools of Statutory Interpretation

Let's recap. Statutory interpretation begins with the text of the rule, the most authoritative source of meaning.[62] Remember that if there is no ambiguity in the terms, plain meaning controls—but ambiguity will almost always be present in cases headed for litigation. To ensure a complete analysis, break the rule into its component parts (see Part A). This part of the chapter explains how to then analyze those pieces of the rule.

Initial Steps: Binding Sources

It may seem counterintuitive, but you should research binding sources that have construed your statutory provision before determining whether the rule contains ambiguous text. This research may be what informs you of the ambiguity in the first instance, and in the best case scenario, has already resolved it for you.

a. Intrinsic Sources — Statutory Definitions and Related Provisions

Because your interpretive effort begins within the statutory text, you should always check whether any of its terms are defined in the statute (note that the definitions section of a statute may be located apart from the provision being construed). If a relevant term is defined, this definition must be applied. Statutory definitions supersede other conflicting sources of meaning and bind all courts interpreting the statute.[63]

To illustrate, let's assume Dana enters a fruit tart baking contest. The contest rules explicitly require the use of fruit. Hoping to score high on creativity, Dana makes a tomato tart. Dana's entry is disqualified by the judges for "lack of fruit."

Does Dana have an argument that disqualification was improper? If, in the fine print of the contest rules, fruit is defined as consisting exclusively of apples,

---

62. *E.g., id.* at 353 (observing that a court "will value more highly a good argument based on the statutory text than a conflicting and equally strong argument based upon the statutory purpose").

63. This discussion assumes that the constitutionality of the statute is not at issue.

blueberries, raspberries, kiwis, and strawberries, then probably not. In this context, "fruit" becomes a "term of art" (a term with a distinct legal meaning). The scientific, dictionary definition of tomato as a fruit holds no water against a definition intrinsic to the rule. The dictionary definition might, however, be relevant to interpreting a more flexible statutory definition, such as "any food that a reasonable person would consider to be 'fruit.'"

Note that other provisions in the same statute could be dispositive of your client's facts. For example, perhaps another rule establishes a minimum age of eighteen for entering the fruit tart contest, and Dana is not yet eighteen. In that situation, it may not make sense to move forward with a challenge to Dana's disqualification, regardless of the statutory definition.[64]

b. Extrinsic Sources

Remember that although the text of the statute trumps any conflicting source of authority (except for a constitution), its meaning may be refined by other binding sources. For example, government agencies with expertise in a particular area, like the Environmental Protection Agency or the Food and Drug Administration, sometimes provide implementing regulations to which courts defer in applying the governing statute.[65]

Courts are also bound by higher-court interpretations of the same statute. Assume that the hypothetical above involved a statute that defined "fruit" in terms of the "reasonable person." If the high court in your jurisdiction held that a reasonable person would consider a tomato a "fruit," a trial court would be bound by that conclusion. For this reason, you must consider binding cases when making a prediction for a client.

Other Tools

If binding sources are not conclusive of meaning in your case, other tools come into play, the most basic of which are listed below. To illustrate how all of these tools of statutory interpretation may be used in practice, we'll use the example of *Yates v. United States*.[66] However, keep in mind that the U.S.

---

64. As a new attorney, make sure you stay within the scope of any assignment given to you by a supervisor. Often the supervisor has reasons for keeping an inquiry narrow.

65. *See* Chevron, U.S.A., Inc. v. Nat. Res. Def. Council, Inc., 467 U.S. 837, 844–45 (1984). The role of administrative regulations in statutory interpretation is otherwise beyond the scope of this textbook.

66. 135 S. Ct. 1074 (2015).

Supreme Court's priorities and process do not perfectly map those of state or other federal courts, due to the diminished constraints of precedents at the Supreme Court level.[67]

The *Yates* case involved the Sarbanes-Oxley Act of 2002, federal legislation prompted by the massive scandal and demise of the Enron Corporation, along with its auditor, Arthur Andersen LLP, which had systematically destroyed incriminating financial documents.[68] The defendant in *Yates* was a commercial fisherman who had been convicted for destroying undersized fish (grouper) to evade federal investigation.[69] The relevant provision of the Act, 18 U.S.C. § 1519, states:

> Whoever knowingly alters, destroys, mutilates, conceals, covers up, falsifies, or makes a false entry in any record, document, or tangible object with the intent to impede, obstruct, or influence the investigation or proper administration of any [United States government] matter....[70]

The question before the Court was whether the fish constituted "tangible object[s]" within the meaning of the statute.[71] A plurality of the Court held that the term "tangible object" did not include fish and reversed the defendant's conviction.[72]

Plain Meaning. As has been noted several times, the plain meaning of statutory text is applied in the absence of ambiguity. But whether an ambiguity exists can itself be the point of contention. This was the situation in *Yates*. The government argued that the term "tangible object" was unambiguous, embracing all relevant physical items—including undersized fish.[73]

The Court disagreed, but the plain meaning argument was succinctly articulated in Justice Kagan's dissent:

> This case raises the question whether the term "tangible object" means the same thing in § 1519 as it means in everyday language—any object

---

67. In other courts, once you have exhausted your research on binding interpretive sources, persuasive precedents remain an important resource for additional guidance.

68. 135 S. Ct. at 1081.

69. *Id.* at 1078.

70. 18 U.S.C. § 1519.

71. 135 S. Ct. at 1081.

72. *Id.*

73. *Id.*

capable of being touched. The answer should be easy: Yes. The term "tangible object" is broad, but clear.[74]

Statutory Context. That words draw meaning from statutory context is widely accepted, even among textualists.[75] Yet agreement on this premise begs the question, as it presupposes agreement that the text is itself ambiguous.[76] As the plurality noted in *Yates*, the ordinary meaning of a term is *usually* the same as its meaning within the statute, but not *always*.[77] Only when the two at least plausibly diverge do interpreters consider the statute's express statement of purpose (if one is provided), surrounding words, surrounding provisions, use of the same terms elsewhere,[78] or even headings.

These types of considerations were cited to support the plurality's conclusion in *Yates* that "tangible object" in § 1519 meant only physical items designed to preserve information, like computers and hard drives—not fish.[79] The provision's caption stated, "Destruction, alteration, or falsification of records in Federal investigations and bankruptcy," and its section title read, "Criminal penalties for altering documents."[80] The Court further observed that the Sarbanes-Oxley Act additions were placed amid Chapter 73's specialized provisions, aimed at corporate fraud and financial audits, not within its

---

74. *Yates*, 135 S. Ct. at 1090–91 (Kagan, J., dissenting). Justice Kagan, joined by Justices Scalia, Kennedy, and Thomas, explained:

> A fish is, of course, a discrete thing that possesses physical form. *See generally* Dr. Seuss, ONE FISH TWO FISH RED FISH BLUE FISH (1960). So the ordinary meaning of the term "tangible object" in § 1519, as no one here disputes, covers fish (including too-small red grouper).

Id. at 1091.

75. *See, e.g.*, King v. Burwell, 135 S. Ct. 2480, 2489 (2015) (advising that words be interpreted "in their context and with a view to their place in the overall statutory scheme" (internal quotations omitted)); United Sav. Ass'n of Texas v. Timbers of Inwood Forest Assocs., Ltd., 484 U.S. 365, 371 (1988) (Scalia, J., dissenting) ("A provision that may seem ambiguous in isolation is often clarified by the remainder of the statutory scheme—because the same terminology is used elsewhere in a context that makes its meaning clear...." (internal citations omitted)).

76. *See, e.g.*, *King*, 135 S. Ct. at 2502 (Scalia, J., dissenting) ("Statutory design and purpose matter only to the extent they help clarify an otherwise ambiguous provision.").

77. *See* 135 S. Ct. at 1082 ("We have several times affirmed that identical language may convey varying content when used in different statutes, sometimes even in different provisions of the same statute." (internal citations omitted)).

78. *See* Smith v. United States, 508 U.S. 223, 233–36 (1993).

79. 135 S. Ct. at 1079.

80. *Id.* at 1083.

broader prohibitions on evidence tampering.[81] The *Yates* dissent rejected the relevance of these contextual clues because it saw no textual ambiguity that would prompt recourse to additional sources of meaning.[82]

Canons of Construction. The canons of construction are a vast set of general rules, originally designed to advise legislatures how a written statute would likely be construed.[83] Often carrying their Latin names, they circulate as "rules of thumb that help courts determine the meaning of legislation,"[84] like the following:

- *Expressio unius:* expression of one thing suggests the exclusion of others.
- *Noscitur a sociis:* interpret a general term to be similar to more specific terms in a series.
- *Ejusdem generis:* interpret a general term to reflect the class of objects reflected in more specific terms accompanying it.

The *Yates* plurality relied on the canon *noscitur a sociis*, to demonstrate that the third term in the series, "record, document, or tangible object," should be interpreted consistent with the specific preceding terms, both of which preserve or record information.[85] Similarly, the Court cited *ejusdem generis*, reasoning that "tangible object" should be interpreted in line with the narrower class occupied by "record" and "document."[86]

Canons of construction are not only linguistic, but substantive in nature, such as the rule of lenity: construe ambiguous criminal statutes in favor of the defendant. The *Yates* opinion cites this canon, too, explaining that a narrow understanding of "tangible object" was appropriate for a criminal statute carrying a potential twenty-year prison term.[87]

The canons of construction were famously examined in 1950 by Karl Llewellyn, a member of the American Legal Realism school of thought, which believed that the constraints of rules were largely illusory, masking the considerable power of judges to determine outcomes in individual cases.[88] To chal-

---

81. *Id.* at 1084. The dissent argued that the surrounding words of the provision supported a wide scope, reinforced by the same phrase appearing in the Model Penal Code. *See id.* at 1092–93 (Kagan, J., dissenting).

82. *See id.* at 1092.

83. William N. Eskridge, Jr. & Philip P. Frickey, *Foreword: Law as Equilibrium*, 108 HARV. L. REV. 26, 65–67 (1994).

84. Conn. Nat'l Bank v. Germain, 503 U.S. 249, 253 (1992).

85. 135 S. Ct. at 1085.

86. *Id.* at 1086–87.

87. *Id.* at 1088.

88. Karl N. Llewellyn, *Remarks on the Theory of Appellate Decisions & the Rules or Cannons About How Statutes Are to Be Construed*, 3 VAND. L. REV. 395, 400 (1950) ("If a

lenge the pretense that any rule could possess a single correct meaning, Llewellyn collected the canons to demonstrate "there are two opposing canons on almost every point."[89] This chart illustrates several such oppositions:[90]

A statute cannot go beyond its text.	To effect its purpose a statute may be implemented beyond its text.
Where design has been distinctly stated no place is left for construction.	Courts have the power to inquire into the real—as distinct from ostensible—purpose.
Titles do not control meaning; preambles do not expand scope; section headings do not change language.	The title may be consulted as a guide when there is doubt or obscurity in the body; preambles may be consulted to determine rationale, and thus the true construction of terms; section headings may be looked upon as part of the statute itself.
A statutory provision requiring liberal construction does not mean disregard of unequivocal requirements of the statute.	Where a rule of construction is provided within the statute itself the rule should be applied.

The myriad presumptions available helps explain why the *Yates* dissent had a parry to the plurality's every thrust. As to the title of the statute, for example, the dissent adopted "the wise rule that the title of a statute and the heading of a section cannot limit the plain meaning of the text."[91] The canons, stated the dissent, must be used "to resolve ambiguity, not create it."[92]

Today, many jurisdictions have codified canons,[93] as well as common law canons. Make sure you use canons grounded in primary sources of law, for

---

statute is to be merged into a going system of law,..., the court must do the merging, and must in so doing take account of the policy of the statute—or else substitute its own version of such policy. Creative reshaping of the net result is thus inevitable.").

89. *Id.* at 401.

90. *Id.* at 401–06.

91. *Yates,* 135 S. Ct. at 1094 (internal citation omitted).

92. *Id.* at 1097.

93. *See, e.g.,* N.Y. STAT. LAW §92 (McKinney) ("The primary consideration of the courts in the construction of statutes is to ascertain and give effect to the intention of the Legislature."); *id.* §94 ("The legislative intent is to be ascertained from the words and language used, and the statutory language is generally construed according to its natural and most obvious sense, without resorting to an artificial or forced construction."); *id.* §96 ("A basic consideration in the interpretation of a statute is the general spirit and purpose underlying

example a "statute on statutes"[94] or case law that applies a canon in the context of the statute being construed.[95]

Non-binding case law. Persuasive precedents from your jurisdiction are excellent sources of meaning when they construe the statutory provision at issue. They are most helpful when, in addition to interpreting the same language, the facts are analogous to those of your client, they are well-reasoned, or they reflect a larger body of support. Despite the Supreme Court's place at the top of the judicial food chain, the dissent in *Yates* invoked the persuasive weight of precedent to compare the statutory text to the same in a witness tampering statute which "encompasses no less the bloody knife than the incriminating letter, as all courts have for decades agreed."[96]

Legislative history. Legislative history may offer insights into meaning, in the form of congressional reports, debates, and earlier drafts of the statute in question.[97] Both sides in *Yates* made reference to legislative history in support of their respective arguments.[98] Even if you do not find a source that sheds meaning on the particular terms at issue, legislative history might reveal less direct, but still useful, information, e.g., that your statute was modeled after one in a different state; if so, comparing language used or rejected might provide a basis for making inferences about the ambiguous text.

Dictionaries (legal or standard). Although recognized sources of guidance in ascertaining the "plain meaning" of language,[99] keep in mind dictionaries are secondary sources of law. In addition, recall that a plain meaning interpretation of text does not presume that meaning is derived from the term in isolation. As noted in *Yates*, "[w]hether a statutory term is unambiguous,…, does not turn solely on dictionary definitions of its component words," but is determined by "the specific context in which that language is used, and the broader context of the statute as a whole."[100]

* * *

---

its enactment, and that construction is to be preferred which furthers the object, spirit and purpose of the statute.").

94. *See, e.g.,* N.Y. Stat. Law §§ 91–98 (McKinney).

95. *See, e.g.,* United States v. Miller, 161 F.3d 977, 983 (6th Cir. 1998) (discussing *ejusdem generis*).

96. *Yates*, 135 S. Ct. at 1093 (Kagan, J., dissenting) (internal citations omitted).

97. *See, e.g.,* Pub. Citizen v. U.S. Dep't of Justice, 491 U.S. 440, 461–63 (1989) (consulting congressional reports).

98. *See Yates*, 135 S. Ct. at 1084–85, 1093–94 (discussing legislative history).

99. *See generally* Jason Weinstein, *Against Dictionaries: Using Analogical Reasoning to Achieve a More Restrained Textualism*, 38 U. Mich. J.L. Reform 649 (2005).

100. *Yates*, 135 S. Ct. at 1081–82 (internal citations omitted).

In practice, you generally will not use all of the methods in every case, and they may not be equally acceptable to courts. But the foundational inventory above offers the tools attorneys turn to time and again when interpreting a statute. Mastering these concepts will give you a toolbox to reach into whenever the statutory language provides no clear answers.

C. Rules in Precedents

In addition to rules found in statutory text, the law is also made up of court-made rules. This section introduces that mercurial breed of rule and explains the process of synthesizing a rule from precedents.

1. Court-Made Rules

Judges decide cases; rule-making is not their charge. Yet, a single decision may send the law into a tailspin, reorienting its trajectory. *MacPherson v. Buick Motor Co.*[101] was such a case. In 1916, then-Judge (and later Supreme Court Justice) Benjamin Cardozo upended the landscape of products liability law by jettisoning a longstanding requirement (known as "privity of contract") that plaintiffs injured by products could only bring suit against the person from whom they purchased the product, such as a retailer or distributor.[102] Post-*MacPherson*, plaintiffs could bring claims against a manufacturer of a defective product even if the plaintiff did not buy the product directly from that manufacturer and therefore had never entered into a contract with the manufacturer. Despite its radical impact, the origins of the case were personal and specific: Donald MacPherson was injured driving a Buick with a defective wheel.[103]

While rules are birthed from the particular facts of the case, it is their generalized form that governs future cases. As Cass Sunstein noted, "[a]lmost any judgment about a particular case depends on the use of principles or reasons. Any principles or reasons are, by their very nature, broader than the case for which they are designed."[104] Combine Sunstein's observation with the principle of *stare decisis*, and you get court-made rules that constrain fu-

---

101. 217 N.Y. 382 (1916).

102. *See id.* at 389–90 ("We have put aside the notion that the duty to safeguard life and limb, when the consequences of negligence may be foreseen, grows out of contract and nothing else.").

103. *Id.* at 384–85.

104. Cass R. Sunstein, *Problems with Rules*, 83 CALIF. L. REV. 953, 957 (1995).

ture courts. The common law thus advances through an accretive process, each case reinforcing or altering the shape of the law, whether by drastic lurch or slight shift.

Further, recall that court-made rules are not restricted to the world of common law (see Part A). Cases develop rules to interpret, apply, or explain broader rules enacted by legislatures or other authorities. Take the Sherman Act, which has provided for over a century that, "Every contract, combination in the form of trust or otherwise, or conspiracy, in restraint of trade or commerce among the several States, or with foreign nations, is declared to be illegal."[105] When it came to applying this antitrust provision in 1911, the Supreme Court decided that a "restraint of trade" meant an "undue restraint" of trade.[106] Once the two types of restraint were distinguished, courts developed a "rule of reason analysis" to root out the prohibited kind.[107] Over the years, a vast network of court-made rules continues to evolve, as is true in many areas of law, despite the primary text of the rule remaining unchanged.[108]

With this background in mind, we turn to rule synthesis.

2. Synthesizing a Rule from Precedents

Because court-made rules spring from particular factual scenarios, courts may articulate the same rule differently. A court might apply a rule without explicitly stating it at all. Rule synthesis involves examining precedents to find the common principle that explains the outcome in each one. And it involves articulating a rule that may not have been explicitly recognized as a rule.

Initially, rule synthesis may feel like "making up" the law. It is not a function of invention, however, but of inductive logic: using discrete data points to formulate a broader hypothesis. Inductive logic requires generalizing from

---

105. E.g., 15 U.S.C. § 1.

106. Standard Oil Co. of N.J. v. United States, 221 U.S. 1, 60 (1911); *see also* Bd. of Trade of City of Chicago v. United States, 246 U.S. 231, 238 (1918) (observing that, literally speaking, "[e]very agreement concerning trade, every regulation of trade, restrains").

107. *See* United States v. Topco Assocs., Inc., 405 U.S. 596, 607 (1972) ("An analysis of the reasonableness of particular restraints includes consideration of the facts peculiar to the business in which the restraint is applied, the nature of the restraint and its effects, and the history of the restraint and the reasons for its adoption." (internal citation omitted)).

108. *See, e.g.,* Richard A. Posner, *The Jurisprudence of Skepticism*, 86 Mich. L. Rev. 827, 835 (1988) ("The body of rules that make up, for example, constitutional law, antitrust law, and tort law have changed greatly in the last century, even though the Constitution and the Sherman Act (1890) have not changed much and torts remains mostly a common-law field. It is the judges who have changed the rules.").

the particulars. If, for example, you sit by the ocean and watch three fish, of different shapes and sizes, swimming under water, you might hypothesize that fish can breathe underwater. The conclusion would be uncertain, but that's the nature of inductive logic—its conclusions are provisional. However, short of an established scientifically-validated truth, a probable rule is still useful.

So too in law. Although rules based on inductive reasoning are not absolute, they serve a key role in the law's development.[109] New decisions continuously provide new sets of particulars that shape or reshape existing principles, usually incrementally but sometimes drastically, as in the *MacPherson* case referenced above.[110] Many doctrinal courses use inductive reasoning in showing how a rule evolved through a series of particular cases, each one adding to the mix until the contours of a rule become visible. Lawyers play a key role in shaping court-made rules because they design the prototypes from which the court selects. Good lawyering, then, requires knowing how to construct a rule using inductive logic.[111]

To synthesize a rule, look to the "determinative facts" in each case. A determinative fact is one that drives the outcome; without it the result would be different. But how do you know which facts are determinative? And how narrow or generalized should the rule be? Maybe all living creatures can breathe underwater. Maybe only the three kinds of fish witnessed can breathe underwater.

With only a single example, a generalized inference is more speculative. If you just saw just one fish swimming, for example, a hypothesis that all fish breathe underwater would be a stretch. Consider *Donoghue v. Stevenson*, a famous British case from 1932.[112] In *Donoghue*, the plaintiff ordered a ginger beer in a café, which was served in an opaque bottle.[113] She drank until noticing

---

109. *See* Anita Schnee, *Logical Reasoning "Obviously,"* 3 J. LEGAL WRITING INST. 105, 116 (1997) (noting that inductive reasoning has an indeterminate nature, yet "is nevertheless an essential part of the law's growing process").

110. As Frederick Schauer has observed, the law is not a "closed system," like a game of chess, but rather like a game whose rules can never be fully determined. *See* SCHAUER, *supra* note 28, at 5–6.

111. *See* Ruggero J. Aldisert, Stephen Clowney & Jeremy D. Peterson, *Logic for Law Students: How to Think Like a Lawyer*, 69 U. PITT. L. REV. 1, 15 (2007) ("Notwithstanding its shortcomings, inductive generalization remains a vital tool, because the ability to shape persuasive legal arguments when no clear precedent exists is often what separates a star attorney from your run-of-the-mill ambulance chaser.").

112. Donoghue v. Stevenson [1932] A.C. 562 (H.L.).

113. *Id.* at 562.

a decomposed snail at the bottom, and then suffered shock and acute gastroenteritis.[114] The House of Lords found the manufacturer liable in negligence.[115]

The *Donoghue* holding contradicted the prevailing common law rule, which
generally protected manufacturers from defective product suits brought by injured third-party consumers for lack of a direct contractual relationship—the
same rule earlier capsized in New York, by the *MacPherson* case.[116] Although
deviation from prior law was apparent, the breadth of the new rule was uncertain. Was the entire common law universe of manufacturer protection oblit-
erated? Or was the door merely cracked for certain species of claims, e.g.,
defective food products? Without an explicit pronouncement from the court,
a multitude of possibilities existed.[117]

Assume that the *Donoghue* opinion contained no hint of reasoning, and
a new case came about, this time triggered by a snail discovered in a relatively
transparent bottle of seltzer—the consumer didn't notice until too late, suf-
fering shock and gastroenteritis. Is the manufacturer liable under the rule applied in *Donoghue*? The plaintiff's attorney would argue yes, here was
effectively the same product and injury. The manufacturer, however, could
argue no, the rule in *Donoghue* was limited to defects that are hidden from
the consumer's eye, as with the opaque bottle. Both arguments would be
plausible.

Each different fact scenario tests a rule's boundaries, potentially narrowing
or broadening them. For example, assume the next case involved a television
that contained defective internal wiring and exploded when the consumer
turned it on at home, resulting in minor skin burns and damage to the car-
peting. Again, the case could be decided in favor of the plaintiff under a generalized reading of the *Donoghue* rule. Or the next court might reject the claim,
limiting *Donoghue* to food manufacturers or more extreme physical injury.

Once several courts have ruled on a topic, the attorney facing a new set of
facts must consider this body of precedent to synthesize a rule. To find the determinative facts, search for those that consistently appear in cases reaching
the same outcome. In the fish example, all three cases involved different types
of fish, none of which surfaced for oxygen. From here, you can hypothesize
that the next fish you encounter will likewise demonstrate a capacity to breathe
underwater.

---

114. *Id.* at 566.
115. *Id.* at 623.
116. *See* MacPherson v. Buick Motor Inc., 217 N.Y. 382 (1916).
117. *See* Melvin A. Eisenberg, *The Principles of Legal Reasoning in the Common Law, in*
Common Law Theory 81, 88–89 (Douglas E. Edlin, ed., 2007).

Returning to products liability, let's say your client seeks recovery from the manufacturer of an autonomous robot vacuum cleaner; he turned it on and then left the house to do errands. In his absence, an unseen defect caused the robot to explode and burn down his home. The instructions cautioned against leaving the robot on by itself but say nothing about a possible explosion.

Finding no statute on point, your research reveals three relevant cases. To synthesize the rule, consider creating a chart that links the potentially determinative facts to a specific holding:

Case	Facts	Holding
Donoghue	• Beverage sold in opaque container • Snail at bottom • Plaintiff suffers shock and acute gastroenteritis.	Manufacturer liable.
Case 2	• Beverage sold in transparent container • Snail at bottom • Plaintiff suffers shock and acute gastroenteritis.	Manufacturer not liable.
Case 3	• Television • Internal wiring causes explosion • Minor burns/property damage.	Manufacturer liable.

The rule that you synthesize from these cases should have the following qualities: (1) easy to understand; (2) easy to apply; and (3) consistent with the relevant authorities.[118] Let's test the following rule:

> "Manufacturers are liable for products containing hidden defects that cause injury to consumers."

First, this rule seems easy to understand because the language is straightforward. Compare this to a rule like, "A manufacturer of a product that was negligently produced and ultimately results in a consumer who is injured due to a defect can be liable when the defect is not necessarily obviously seen by the user, though the degree to which the defect is visible may not be quantifiable at this stage." A rule like this would be cumbersome for a reader to process, which makes it less useful.

---

118. *See* Paul Figley, *Teaching Rule Synthesis with Real Cases*, 61 J. LEGAL EDUC. 245, 247 (2011).

Second, the rule is easy to apply because it offers guidance in determining an outcome for the particular fact scenario you face: liability will ensue if the defect was hidden. Applying the rule to our facts, the issue becomes whether a defect that was not visible to the eye was "hidden," even though the instruction manual cautioned against leaving the product out of sight. Compare that to a rule like, "Manufacturers may be held liable in negligence for defective products, like television wiring or a bottled beverage." This rule is easy to understand, but what does it mean for the facts of your case? The rule is difficult to apply because it does not indicate which of your facts are important or why.

Third, the rule is consistent with the relevant authorities. Ideally, the rule should be as tailored as possible in guiding the reader to the outcome, while still embracing all relevant case law. A good way to ensure your rule is accurate is to go back and test it against the facts of each case. Is the outcome still the same? Then the rule is solid. If your rule cannot account for a case, you'll need to rethink the rule — much as your theory about fish breathing underwater would be undone by a fish that continually resurfaces to catch its breath.

Compare our proposed rule to this rule: "Manufacturers are liable for all product defects that injure consumers." That rule does not account for Case 2, which rejected manufacturer liability when the same defect was packaged in a transparent bottle.

In a similar vein, make sure that your research is thorough so you don't generalize from an insufficient number of examples and inadvertently mischaracterize the law.[119] A flawed rule will result in an inaccurate analysis or a weak argument.

The boundaries of rule synthesis may feel elusive at the beginning, but you will eventually develop a sense of an acceptable range of rules based on the cases under consideration. As you wade into the sea of particulars and begin crafting your generalizations, here are some common pitfalls to avoid.

1. **The quotation.** Although it will be tempting to extract a court's language for your rule because it cannot be criticized as incorrect, doing so may unduly limit your rule. Assume you find the following quotation in Case 1: "When a food manufacturer sells a defective product, the poisoned consumer must have recourse." That quotation may support the holding of Case 1, but it is not a synthesized rule. It doesn't account for the holding in Case 2 (food manufacturer,

---

119. Judge Aldisert called this the "Fallacy of Hasty Generalization." *See* Aldisert, *supra* note 111, at 14–15.

poisoned consumer, no liability), or Case 3 (no food manufacturer, no poisoning, but manufacturer liable).

2. **The overly broad rule.** A broad rule may be perfectly accurate, e.g., "Manufacturers can be held liable in negligence." Yet this rule is practically useless for predicting the outcome of the present case or crafting an argument. An effective rule tells the reader when a manufacturer will be held liable in negligence, specifying the characteristics that support this result—not simply the possibility of the result itself.

3. **The fact aggregation.** Another common error is failing to abstract a common principle and instead presenting an unwieldy aggregation of facts, such as: "A manufacturer is liable in negligence under a variety of circumstances, including when a beverage contains animal remains, so long as the bottle is opaque, and when a television set explodes, if the explosion resulted from defective internal wiring." This rule doesn't succinctly convey the common principle that leads to manufacturer liability, but rather asks the readers to perform the inductive analysis themselves.

4. **The circular rule.** The circular rule basically states that the rule is satisfied when the rule is satisfied. For example, "Manufacturers may be held liable in negligence for defective products that injure consumers when they negligently manufacture defective products that result in consumer injury." A rule should not end at its starting point, but rather relay the essential condition for meeting it.

Keep in mind that even a sound rule may be challenged in an adversarial situation as overly broad or narrow. Even with several cases on point, competing characterizations may be plausible, depending, for example, on whether a precedent's reasoning is considered dicta or essential to the holding. Learning the basics of good rule synthesis will help prepare you for more sophisticated uses down the road.

As a final point, remember that rule synthesis, like other aspects of legal analysis, will be informed by the hierarchy of authority. This means that the cases selected to support the rule should reflect binding case law in your jurisdiction, if possible, and otherwise the most persuasive, relevant cases available. The citations that follow a rule of law tell the reader whether the rule *must* be followed or *should* be followed as a matter of *stare decisis*. When relying on persuasive authority, citing more than one case will strengthen the weight of the stated rule.

Chapter 5

Deductive Reasoning

Previous chapters helped you derive and understand the rules found in legal authorities. Now that you've uncovered those rules, you must learn how to use them in your own analysis.[1] Deductive reasoning, also called "rule-based reasoning," is the backbone of this kind of logic-based analysis,[2] as explained in this chapter.

A. The Deductive Paradigm

Deduction is a form of logic premised on the following principle: what is true for the universal is true for the particular.[3] The power of deductive logic lies in the syllogism, a structure whereby a conclusion is derived from two known premises.

---

1. KARL LLEWELLYN, THE BRAMBLE BUSH: THE CLASSIC LECTURES ON THE LAW AND LAW SCHOOL 6 (2008) (noting that "the getting of the judge to do a thing is in considerable measure the art of finding what rules are available to urge upon them, and of how to urge them to accomplish your result").

2. *See, e.g.*, Ruggero J. Aldisert, Stephen Clowney & Jeremy D. Peterson, *Logic for Law Students: How to Think Like a Lawyer*, 69 U. PITT. L. REV. 1, 2 (2007) ("Perhaps 90 percent of legal issues can be resolved by deduction, so the importance of understanding this type of reasoning cannot be overstated."); Richard A. Posner, *The Jurisprudence of Skepticism*, 86 MICH. L. REV. 827, 832 (1988) (asserting that "[t]he vast majority of legal questions can be and are resolved syllogistically").

3. *See, e.g.*, Aldisert, *supra* note 2, at 4 (citing JOSEPH GERARD BRENNAN, A HANDBOOK OF LOGIC 64 (1957)).

All humans are mortal. (major premise)
Socrates is a human. (minor premise)
Therefore, Socrates is mortal. (conclusion)

The beauty of the syllogism lies in its certainty. If a major premise is true, and the minor premise is true, then the conclusion *must* be true. The major premise lays out the universal circumstance: every being that fits within the category of "human" has the characteristic of being "mortal." The minor premise then shows that the particular being at stake here—Socrates—fits within the category of human. Therefore, he *must* possess the characteristic of mortality.

In a legal syllogism, the major premise corresponds to the legal rule, and the minor premise provides the facts of the case at hand. To work effectively, the legal rule must lay out the universal circumstance, that everything that falls into category x also has characteristic y. The minor premise then shows that the facts of our particular case are x; the legal conclusion must therefore be y.[4]

Here's an example of how this looks in a legal context:

Drivers of vehicles who do not stop at red lights violate the law. (major premise)
Leia did not stop at a red light. (minor premise)
Leia violated the law. (conclusion)

The x here—the category—is drivers who do not stop at red lights. Any individual who falls into category x also has characteristic y: she violates the law. The minor premise shows that our fact z fits within category x. Therefore, z also has characteristic y.

If those x's and z's make your head hurt, here's an alternate way to think about it: Deductive logic moves from general to specific, like an inverted triangle:

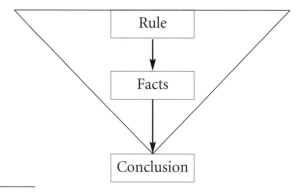

_____

4. *See, e.g.*, Anita Schnee, *Logical Reasoning "Obviously,"* 3 J. Legal Writing Inst. 105, 106–09 (1997).

If certain facts fit within the rule, if they present a specific circumstance covered by the rule, then moving from the general to the specific leads to a legal conclusion.

You may recall from Chapter 4 that rule synthesis works by induction, an inversion of the process depicted above. With inductive reasoning, the particular serves as a springboard for generalizing outward (flip the triangle for a visual representation). Seeing several fish breathing underwater leads to a rule that all fish breathe underwater.

These two forms of reasoning are often combined in legal analysis. If legal authorities state no direct rule, a lawyer can craft one by synthesizing the results from multiple authorities. She then applies that newly-synthesized rule as the major premise in the syllogism outlined above.

While combining these two forms of reasoning is common, it can also lead to potential missteps. Deductive reasoning remains powerful insofar as both of its premises are true, but inductive reasoning introduces at least a modicum of uncertainty to the major premise. Seeing several fish breathing underwater does not eliminate the possibility that certain kinds of fish do not breathe underwater; all it means is that, in your experience, all fish breathe underwater.

The legal syllogism, reliant as it is on rule synthesis, is thus more commonly flawed than the traditional logical syllogism. This is why in many cases, more than one syllogism can exist and be valid; the decision-maker must choose between them. Thus, despite the problems with the legal syllogism, to effectively analyze or argue a legal problem, you must have a strong grasp on the syllogism that leads to your conclusion.

Most judicial opinions are reducible to syllogisms, although they may not be obviously stated in the text of the decisions.[5] Consider the following:

Brown v. Board of Education[6]
Unequal educational facilities are not permitted under the Constitution. (major premise)
A separate educational facility for black children is inherently unequal. (minor premise)
Therefore a separate educational facility for black children is not permitted under the Constitution. (conclusion)[7]

---

5. *See* Aldisert, *supra* note 2, at 3.
6. 347 U.S. 483 (1954).
7. This example is provided in Aldisert, *supra* note 2, at 5 (citing *Brown*, 347 U.S. at 493–95).

Yates v. United States[8]

Destroying tangible objects to obstruct a federal investigation violates the Sarbanes-Oxley Act. (major premise)

A fish is not a tangible object under the Sarbanes-Oxley Act. (minor premise)

Destroying fish to obstruct a federal investigation does not violate the Sarbanes-Oxley Act. (conclusion)

Florida v. Reilly[9]

Under the Constitution, the police are entitled to observe a private home's backyard without a search warrant if they do so from a public vantage point where they have a right to be. (major premise)

The view from a helicopter flying at 400 feet is a public vantage point where the police have a right to be. (minor premise)

Therefore, the police were not required to obtain a search warrant to view the contents of the defendant's backyard greenhouse from a helicopter. (conclusion)

But if you read these opinions, you may not see these premises explicitly formulated. Syllogisms rarely jump off the pages of judicial opinions. Rather, they are obscured in verbiage, buried under mounds of facts, and drowned out by the complex law they seek to order. Not only can extraneous text overwhelm the syllogism, but often parts of the syllogism have gone missing. Rather than stated, they are assumed.

Sometimes a major premise has been omitted by virtue of unquestionably shared knowledge (the technical term for such a syllogism is "enthymeme"),[10] but omissions may also disguise faulty reasoning and tenuous assumptions. To avoid tripping into the latter category, make sure all parts of your syllogism are present and accounted for on the page. Dispense with the notion that stating obvious premises or connections will appear simpleminded and unsophisticated, a common misconception among new legal writers. Rather, your time spent researching the relevant law and thinking about how it applies to the facts creates an illusion of obviousness that is lost on a reader who has not made the same cognitive investment. Make your logic explicit.

Syllogisms may also be concealed in legal argument because they require multiple logical steps to reach the conclusion. The *Yates v. United States* syllogism

---

8. 135 S. Ct. 1074 (2015).

9. 488 U.S. 445 (1989).

10. *See* Aldisert, *supra* note 2, at 7–8 (suggesting that the use of enthymemes is fairly common in legal reasoning).

provided above, for example, contains a precursor syllogism, with the question of the proper major premise dominating the Supreme Court's opinion:[11]

A tangible object means one used to record or preserve information.
A fish is not used to record or preserve information.
Therefore, a fish is not a tangible object under the Sarbanes-Oxley Act.

Destroying tangible objects to obstruct a federal investigation violates the Sarbanes-Oxley Act.
A fish is not a tangible object under the Sarbanes-Oxley Act.
Destroying fish to obstruct a federal investigation does not violate the Sarbanes-Oxley Act.

B. Using Deductive Reasoning

Because syllogistic reasoning is so compelling, and disputes so often boil down to the validity or relative merits of competing syllogisms, you should use this form in constructing legal arguments.[12] A clear structure is essential, but that structure is only as good as the logic it's built with. Here, we'll parse some fundamental principles for composing strong syllogisms and highlight common flaws and weaknesses.

1. Putting Together a Syllogism

First, a strong deductive argument requires a well-supported major premise. In law, logic's "universal truth" is a rule supported by binding authority. Just as the babysitter is not expected to observe a rule that children under ten may stay up until midnight if it's scrawled in crayon and presented by giggling seven-year-olds, your rule requires citations to authorities for credibility. Even an impeccably-crafted syllogism will be a failing argument if your rule cites secondary

---

11. *See* 135 S. Ct. 1074 (2015).

12. *E.g.*, Aldisert, *supra* note 2, at 5 ("Whenever possible, make the arguments in your briefs and memos in the form of syllogisms."); Antonin Scalia & Bryan A. Garner, Making Your Case: The Art of Persuading Judges 41 (2008) ("The most rigorous form of logic, and hence the most persuasive, is the syllogism."). For one example, see 44 Liquormart, Inc. v. Rhode Island, 517 U.S. 484, 511 (1996) ("[W]e fail to see how that syllogism requires the conclusion that the State's power to regulate commercial *activity* is 'greater' than its power to ban truthful, nonmisleading commercial *speech*.").

authority while your opponent cites law. Although you may be forced to rely on some persuasive or otherwise non-ideal authorities for your rule, remember that the weaker your authorities, the more vulnerable the rule is to attack.[13]

Second, a major premise must be accurate for the ultimate conclusion to be correct.[14] Say you arranged to meet your friend at a café but insisted she leave her ever-present pug Ernestine at home because you recall seeing a sign in the window stating "No Dogs Allowed." At the café, you realize the sign actually says "Dogs Allowed." Your friend will be unhappy with an outcome premised on a false rule. An adversary would be quick to point out an erroneous major premise (e.g., the statute is misquoted or misinterpreted, the synthesized rule fails to account for a key case), and your client would naturally be displeased with an incorrect prediction or argument.

However, errors should be distinguished from the inalterable reality of existing law. If your major premise has been constructed through rule synthesis, for example, it carries the inherent weaknesses of inductive reasoning. But a synthesized major premise is still better than none.

Third, your major premise should be certain, in the sense of establishing a rule fully applicable to the relevant class. A common flaw in syllogistic reasoning is using a major premise that although true, does not embrace the whole class. As a result, the subject of the minor premise may or may not fall within the designated category. Fallacious logic of this kind is often identifiable through terms like "some," "certain," "sometimes," "many," as follows:

Many restaurants do not allow dogs on the premises.
Twelve Dogs is a restaurant.
Therefore, dogs are not allowed at Twelve Dogs.

Although the minor premise fits within the category covered by the major premise, a restaurant, the major premise is riddled with holes. As a result, the conclusion is unsound. A variation on this flaw may occur in a minor premise. Again, both major and minor premises are true, but they do not necessarily connect because the minor premise refers only to "some" members.

---

13. *See* Ross Guberman, Point Made: How to Write Like the Nation's Top Advocates 159–62 (2d ed. 2014) (citing examples from briefs).

14. *See, e.g.*, Brief of the Am. Fed'n of Labor and Congress of Indus. Org. and the Bhd. of Maint. of Way Emp'r Div., Int'l Bhd. of Teamsters as Amicus Curiae in Support of Respondent at 13, Burlington N. Santa Fe Ry. Co. v. White, 548 U.S. 53 (2006) (No. 05-259), 2006 WL 622124, at *13 ("This syllogism fails at its first step, because the Railway's premise is wrong.").

All dogs are mammals.
Some mammals can fly.
Therefore, dogs can fly.

Fourth, even if your major premise is well-supported, accurate, and certain, the minor premise must belong to the category addressed by the major premise. This fallacy can be particularly tricky to spot when the minor premise reflects a shared characteristic of the category, as opposed to membership in the category:

Dogs are not allowed in the restaurant.
Bronte is not allowed in the restaurant.
Therefore, Bronte is a dog.

All tennis champions practice a lot.
Vanessa practices tennis a lot.
Therefore, Vanessa is a tennis champion.

Nothing in the above examples precludes the conclusions from being true (Bronte might be a dog, and Vanessa might be a tennis champion), but if so, the conclusions have not been proven deductively. That is, the relationship between the premises does not require the conclusion.

Fifth, make sure that all pieces in a deductive chain are covered—and preferably made explicit. For example:

An enforceable contract requires that the offer is accepted.
Francisco accepted the offer implied by the advertisement.
Therefore, Francisco entered an enforceable contract.

This syllogism implies an antecedent deductive step that establishes the legal assumption contained in the minor premise: that an offer implied in an advertisement qualifies as an offer to enter into a contract. The deductive tower could collapse in the event of a rule stating, "An advertisement qualifies as a binding offer to contract only when its terms are explicit and non-negotiable."

To demonstrate your logic is correct, you may need to use a two-tiered syllogism (or more), e.g.:

An advertisement qualifies as a binding offer when its terms are explicit and non-negotiable.
Company Z's advertisement stated in explicit, non-negotiable terms that if 900,000 box tops from Moony Oats cereal were collected, it would send the consumer on a trip to the moon.
Therefore, Company Z's advertisement created a binding offer to contract.

An enforceable contract requires that an offer is accepted.

Francisco accepted the offer in Company Z's advertisement by submitting 900,000 box tops from Moony Oats cereal.

Therefore, Francisco entered into an enforceable contract with Company Z.

Finally, although negative premises can produce a negative conclusion, avoid using negative premises to produce a positive conclusion.[15] To illustrate, the following syllogism rests on two negative premises yet states a positive conclusion:

Minors cannot enter into valid contracts.

Sondra is not a minor.

Therefore, Sondra entered into a valid contract.

The positive conclusion, Sondra's valid contract, is a logical fallacy. This is so because even if Sondra's age does not invalidate the contract, any number of other factors might affect its validity. The relationship between the negative premises does not yield enough information to compel a positive conclusion.

The two negative premises, however, would be enough to deliver a valid negative conclusion, as in:

Minors cannot enter into valid contracts.

Sondra is not a minor.

Therefore, the contract is not invalid on account of Sondra's age.

However, notice how limited the conclusion above is, even if logically sound. Positive premises offer much stronger bases for deductive reasoning—a point to keep in mind when articulating rules.

Further, even when only one of the premises is negative, the conclusion cannot be positive. For example:

Dogs are not allowed in the restaurant.

Dumbledore is a cat.

Therefore, Dumbledore is allowed in the restaurant.

Here, again, the negative major premise precludes a positive conclusion about whether Dumbledore is permitted in the restaurant. The major premise provides so little information in relation to the minor premise that a valid conclusion must be exceedingly narrow:

---

15. *See generally* Stephen M. Rice, *False Persuasion, Superficial Heuristics, and the Power of Logical Form to Test the Integrity of Legal Argument*, 34 Pace L. Rev. 76 (2014) (discussing the "fallacy of negative premises").

Dogs are not allowed in the restaurant.
Dumbledore is a cat.
Therefore, Dumbledore will not be barred from the restaurant for
being a dog.

There are many other ways for legal syllogisms to wither under attack, but
the principles and warnings listed above should help you root them out and
become acquainted with using strong analytical structure in your own writing.
This is not to say that employing a syllogism will necessarily win an argument.
As noted, competing syllogisms are the norm in difficult cases, which means
that just as often, deductive logic may not be "right" in the eyes of the law. But,
as observed by Judge Ruggero Aldisert, even if good reasoning is not always
right, faulty reasoning "can never be right."[16]

C. Deductive Reasoning in Context

Throughout the chapter, we have observed the power of deductive reasoning
to cast a conclusion as an imperative. At the extremes, deductive reasoning is
equated with formalism, a theory that venerates rules over any other factor in
decision-making, for purposes of achieving objective and predictable results.
Formalism thus implies syllogistic reasoning, but the term is also used pejo-
ratively, to suggest overreliance on rules at the expense of fairness. But even
formalists do not believe that law is a science or math equation, as it was popularly framed in the nineteenth century.[17]

Among the jurists revolutionizing law in the early twentieth century by re-
jecting the scientific model was Oliver Wendell Holmes, who said:

> The life of the law has not been logic; it has been experience. The felt
> necessities of the time, the prevalent moral and political theories, in-
> tuitions of public policy, avowed or unconscious, even the prejudices
> which judges share with their fellow-men, have had a good deal more
> to do than the syllogism in determining the rules by which men should
> be governed.[18]

---

16. Aldisert, *supra* note 2, at 22.

17. *See, e.g.*, Stephen M. Feldman, *From Premodern to Modern American Jurisprudence:
The Onset of Positivism*, 50 Vand. L. Rev. 1387, 1428–34 (1997) (discussing the "legal
science" of Christopher Columbus Langdell, in which law was viewed as a set of freestanding
principles, that lawyers must discover).

18. Oliver Wendell Holmes, The Common Law 1 (1881).

In a refutation of formalism, scholars in the American Legal Realism school of thought believed that rules and deductive reasoning offered a mere pretense of objectivity. Syllogisms, they believed, were subterfuge for decisions based on a judge's values, experience, policy concerns, and social biases.[19] Many jurists today integrate social values, morality, and other factors into their reasoning—to varying degrees.

And yet, our current awareness of certain inescapable contingencies has diminished neither the prevalence nor import of deductive reasoning. Why? One explanation can be found in Benjamin Cardozo's rejoinder to Holmes: "[l]ogical consistency does not cease to be a good because it is not the supreme good."[20] Logical consistency remains central to the values of the American legal system, regardless of your faith in the objectivity of deductive reasoning or how it gets balanced against other factors.

Importantly, rule-based reasoning is not the death-knell of creative lawyering, as it may seem at first blush. To the contrary, it is a powerful tool of advocacy. Because courts seize on deductive logic to justify their conclusions, your ability to craft structured syllogisms increases your capacity to assess, predict, and persuade.

---

19. *See* Wilson Huhn, The Five Types of Legal Argument 57–63 (3d ed. 2014) (summarizing historical episode of realism); Brian Leiter, *Rethinking Legal Realism: Toward a Naturalized Jurisprudence*, 76 Tex. L. Rev. 267, 275 (1997) (summarizing legal realism's core claim as, "judges reach decisions based on what they think would be fair on the facts of the case, rather than on the basis of the applicable rules of law").

20. Benjamin N. Cardozo, The Nature of the Judicial Process 32 (1921).

Chapter 6

Analogical Reasoning

Your friend Bob sends out an invitation to a potluck feast. In her emailed RSVP, Sylvia writes, "So excited for this! I'll bring along a fruit dish for dessert." She arrives with a tomato and goat cheese torte. Unhappiness ensues.

Bob is peeved because he believes Sylvia broke her promise to bring a fruit dish. He envisioned an apple pie or peaches with ice cream. Sylvia disagrees; she knows that tomatoes are agriculturally classified as fruits. Regardless, she thinks, Bob has no right to be upset because the dessert is delicious.

The friends turn to you at the end of the dinner party. Who is right? Is a tomato a fruit or a vegetable?

The process you used to reach an answer may have gone something like this: Well, a tomato has seeds like apples and peaches. Sylvia is right; it's technically a fruit.

Or like this: A tomato is usually served with a main course, like carrots or potatoes, not as a dessert. It has a savory taste, not a sweet one. Of course Bob should be mad; a tomato's a vegetable.[1]

If you followed either of these lines of thought, you reasoned by analogy. It is a form of reasoning that is commonplace; we use it every day to make decisions. And it is the aspect of legal reasoning that makes it a unique and distinctive form.

In this chapter, we break down why, exactly, this muddy and controversial form of reasoning has become such a bedrock of legal analysis and provide suggestions for how to construct effective analogies in your own legal writing.

ж   ж   ж

---

1. The Supreme Court answered this very question in the case of *Nix v. Hedden*, 149 U.S. 304 (1893). It decided that even though a tomato was a "fruit of a vine," it was more like a vegetable because it is usually served as part of an entrée, like carrots and potatoes, not as a dessert, like apples or blueberries. *Id.* at 307.

Treat like cases alike.[2] This command of the American legal system enables stability and allows easy cases to be disposed of quickly, often without resort to the adjudicative process. When the result in a present case is moored to the outcomes of past cases, the law remains more predictable, coherent, and, some would argue, fair.[3]

Analogical reasoning is the primary method by which practitioners tie present facts to legal precedent. This kind of formal reasoning is unique to the law — some have called it the hallmark of what makes legal reasoning distinct from other forms of reasoning[4] — but it is also characteristic of much of our informal thought processes. If I like the taste of a filet mignon, then I might safely assume that I will also like the taste of a New York strip. I conclude, based on the fact that both steaks come from the same animal, that they have a similar taste.

This kind of reasoning has a simple structure:

(1) A has characteristic Y;
(2) B has characteristic Y;
(3) A also has characteristic Z;
(4) Because both A and B have Y, B probably also shares characteristic Z.[5]

For our steak example, the analogy would be:

(1) Filet mignon comes from a cow;
(2) New York strip also comes from a cow;
(3) Filet mignon tastes good;
(4) Because both filet mignon and New York strip come from a cow, New York strip will also taste good.

---

2. *See, e.g.*, H.L.A. HART, THE CONCEPT OF LAW 155 (1961).

3. Many theorists have questioned the fairness of this principle, arguing, among other things, that injustice perpetuates itself through the demand that like cases be treated alike. *Stare decisis* guarantees that an unjust result in one case will be replicated again and again. *See, e.g.*, Larry Alexander, *Bad Beginnings*, 145 U. PA. L. REV. 57, 80–86 (1996). While that is certainly a valid argument against the principle, cases are rarely completely "alike," and a thoughtful lawyer can avoid unjust results by arguing that the precedent case is distinguishable from the current case. This chapter gives guidance on how to craft those kinds of arguments.

4. *See, e.g.*, LLOYD L. WEINREB, LEGAL REASON: THE USE OF ANALOGY IN LEGAL ARGUMENT 4 (2d ed. 2016).

5. *See* RUGGERO J. ALDISERT, LOGIC FOR LAWYERS: A GUIDE TO CLEAR LEGAL THINKING 93–94 (3d ed. 1997).

It is easy to say how this logic leads to results that are consistent with precedent. It is also easy to see how quickly this form of reasoning can go awry. In our steak example, for instance, a faulty analogy could be:

(1) Filet mignon comes from a cow;
(2) New York strip comes from a cow;
(3) Filet mignon is pink on the inside when cooked;
(4) Because both filet mignon and New York strip come from a cow, New York strip will also be pink on the inside when cooked.

In fact, another circumstance altogether—your instruction to the chef to cook the filet mignon rare—accounts for its pink coloring. Because the analogy above tagged an irrelevant fact, the analogy does not accurately predict the result.

So too in legal analogies. As H.L.A. Hart said, "[U]ntil it is established what resemblances and differences are relevant, 'Treat like cases alike' must remain an empty form. To fill it, we must know when, for the purposes in hand, cases are to be regarded as alike and what differences are relevant."[6] Because of these weaknesses in the analogical form, because its predictive power is not as strong as deductive or even inductive reasoning, some scholars have questioned its value in legal reasoning, arguing that analogies are simply fig leaves for judges to import their policy preferences into the law.[7] While these objections certainly have merit, they do not change the reality on the ground: An effective lawyer must be able to dexterously deploy analogies to win cases.[8] This chapter helps you do just that.

A. The Judgment of Importance

Let's return to the problem of Sylvia's tomato and goat cheese torte. Both analogies are sound on their faces. Here is Bob's analogy:

(1) Carrots and peas are savory;
(2) Tomatoes are savory;

---

6. H.L.A. HART, THE CONCEPT OF LAW 155 (1961).

7. *See, e.g.,* KARL N. LLEWELLYN, THE BRAMBLE BUSH: THE CLASSIC LECTURES ON THE LAW AND LAW SCHOOL 68–71 (2008); Richard A. Posner, *Reasoning by Analogy,* 91 CORNELL L. REV. 761, 765 (2006); Larry Alexander, *Bad Beginnings,* 145 U. PA. L. REV. 57, 79–80 (1996).

8. Cass R. Sunstein, *On Analogical Reasoning,* 106 HARV. L. REV. 741, 741 (1993) ("Reasoning by analogy is the most familiar form of legal reasoning.... [I]t is a characteristic part of brief-writing and opinion-writing as well.").

(3) Carrots and peas are vegetables;

(4) Therefore, tomatoes are vegetables.

And Sylvia's:

(1) Blueberries and strawberries have seeds;

(2) Tomatoes have seeds;

(3) Blueberries and strawberries are fruits;

(4) Therefore, tomatoes are fruits.

To decide which analogy is more compelling, you must decide whether flavor or seed structure is a more relevant consideration for the dispute. In this context, a dinner party where a guest promised to bring a dessert, flavor likely trumps seeds. Bob's anger is justified.

But in a different context, an agricultural study, say, a tomato's reproductive system would be of primary importance. Seeds would then trump flavor.

The broader context thus controls whether you consider a tomato more like a carrot or like a blueberry. In legal reasoning, too, the purpose of the comparison, the context in which it appears, determines which of two analogies is more compelling. Steven Burton called this the judgment of importance.[9] Each case has some similarities and differences from every other case. An attorney's job is to decide (or argue) that relevant similarities outweigh relevant differences, or vice versa.

And just like the dinner-party context controlled the judgment of importance in our tomato fiasco above, so too does the legal context control the judgment in your legal writing. This legal context is made up of several considerations: (1) the procedural posture, (2) the relevant legal rule, and (3) the policy underlying the legal rule. We discuss each contextual frame below.

1. Procedural Posture

The procedural posture of your case is a crucial contextual consideration because it sets the outer boundaries of relevant facts. As discussed in Chapter 2, certain facts are off-limits at different stages of a litigation. For example, if you are writing a motion to dismiss, arguing that the plaintiff has failed to state a claim upon which relief can be granted under Rule 12(b)(6), then you are limited to the facts as asserted in the complaint. You need to accept these

---

9. Steven J. Burton, An Introduction To Law And Legal Reasoning 57 (3d ed. 2007).

facts as true; your motion will be wildly unsuccessful if you argue the facts in the complaint are false.[10]

An analogy based on facts that are off-limits will fall apart. Thus, it is crucial that you know not only the procedural posture of your own case, but also the procedural posture of the precedent cases. An opinion deciding a post-trial issue in a civil litigation, after the factfinder has resolved factual disputes, is of limited help to a practitioner looking to determine whether her case will survive a motion to dismiss. The circle of available facts is much wider in a post-trial case than it is at the motion-to-dismiss stage, and any analogy between the two is open to attack. The strongest analogies are formed between cases with the same procedural posture; if those cases are unavailable, move on to cases where the procedural standard applied to facts is most similar. The further you travel from the same procedural standard, the more susceptible your analogies are to critique.

2. Legal Rule

While procedural posture is part of the judgment of importance, the applicable legal rule is the North Star of your analogy. Just as the dinner-party context determines whether a tomato is a vegetable or a fruit, so does the legal rule determine whether the facts of your case are similar to or different from the precedent.

Say you were asked to determine whether a court would rule for your client, a farmer, when he failed to deliver a promised bushel of tomatoes to a buyer following a drought. The buyer sued for breach of contract, but the contract contained a provision excusing the parties from their obligations if an "act of God, such as a flood or other natural disaster" intervened. In one previous case, a court ruled for the defendant when the contract contained the same language and the defendant, a farmer, did not deliver a bushel of apples after a hurricane destroyed his apple trees.

One possible legal rule here: An act of God excuses performance. The precedent tells you that a hurricane qualifies as an act of God. The case also notes that the defendant was a farmer, just like your client is a farmer. But nowhere does the legal rule applied in the case mention, or even imply, the defendant's occupation. This common fact is therefore irrelevant. Your focus should be on what qualifies as an act of God, and your analogy should be between droughts and hurricanes.

---

10. *See Iqbal*, 556 U.S. at 678 ("To survive a motion to dismiss, a complaint must contain sufficient factual matter, *accepted as true*, to 'state a claim to relief that is plausible on its face.'" (emphasis added) (internal citation omitted)).

How do you craft such an analogy? Look to the reasoning that led to the result in the precedent case. On the one hand, both hurricanes and droughts are natural disasters that cause significant harm to crops. On the other, a hurricane is a sudden event, while a drought takes place over a long period of time. If the precedent case focused on the extent of the harm caused by natural disasters, then a severe hurricane and a massive drought are analogous. If, however, the judge focused on the sudden nature of the hurricane, then a hurricane and a drought are distinct.

Yet, sometimes, the legal rules and the pertinent precedents do not fully answer the question. Suppose your client had a tank full of reserve water and refused to use it, allowing his tomato crop to wither and die. The precedent case focused only on the massive harm caused by a hurricane and made no mention of whether an individual must take action to protect his crop. Blindly applying the legal rule and the precedent case would lead to an outcome where individuals would be excused from performance when they had the means and ability to fulfill their obligations. When the legal rule and precedents have left a blind spot, then lawyers may turn to the policy underlying the legal rule.

3. Policy

The policy advanced by a legal rule is a third consideration. One possible policy goal in the act-of-God example from above would be to honor the language of the contract as written. The dependability of contracts relies on enforcing the language agreed to by the parties. And since the language here made no mention of a party's duty to offset the harm caused by a natural disaster, the fact that your client did nothing to protect his crops would be irrelevant.

But if the policy goal instead were to ensure that parties to a contract would not be held responsible for their obligations under the contract when disasters beyond their control occur, then the fact your client did not water his plants becomes relevant to the outcome.

Where would a lawyer find the policy undergirding a particular rule? Statutes often contain their purpose in the text itself; if it's not contained there, then a look through the cases interpreting the statute may provide an answer. For common law rules, cases also provide the best resource for determining the policy the rule is supposed to support. If those resources yield nothing, turn to secondary sources, such as treatises, encyclopedias, or law review articles, for clues as to what the legal rule was intended to accomplish.

Sometimes, there is one clearly stated policy rationale for a particular legal rule; these cases are easy. Other times, there is more than one policy rationale, and the potential rationales conflict. When faced with these harder cases, you must choose which principle best satisfies the goals of the legal rule and construct an analogy based on that principle. The strategies for making this choice differ depending on whether you are predicting an outcome or advocating for an outcome. We'll address those strategies in later chapters on objective and persuasive writing.

B. Crafting Analogies and Distinctions

Once a practitioner has made the judgment of importance and has decided whether the similarities or differences between sets of facts control, she must then construct a case comparison to convince others that her analysis is correct. To do this effectively, you must include the facts, reasoning, and holding of the precedent, then compare those facts to the facts of the current case, before concluding that the holding in your case should be the same as in the precedent (or different from the precedent). Case comparisons can either take the form of analogies or distinctions, and your construction of the comparison differs depending on whether you are trying to convince the reader that these cases are alike or different. The difference lies in the level of detail you use to describe the facts of each case.

1. Analogies

With analogies, your goal is to show the reader the connection between the precedent case and the current case. Sometimes, these two sets of facts are identical. These are the easy cases that are often resolved before they ever see the inside of a courtroom (or a lawyer's office). The cases that require lawyerly assistance are often far more difficult. In your writing, your goal is to make concrete the sometimes-abstract connections between precedent and current facts. To do so, you must: (1) identify the specific relevant facts, and (2) generalize out from those facts until the tie between the two cases is clear.

The judgment of importance will help with the first task. You decided which facts were relevant when you decided on the similarities that outweighed the differences. An effective analogy focuses the reader's attention on those facts. The tendency for many beginning law students is to include all the facts they know in the analogy. But experienced attorneys know that technique overwhelms the reader and leads to confusion. Irrelevant facts clog up an analogy; a streamlined analogy that focuses attention only on the relevant information is the goal.

Analogies are at their easiest when the two sets of facts closely track one another. When one farmer milks his neighbor's cow without permission, it's easy to draw the connection between that case and the next farmer-milking-cow case that comes along. But those easy cases are usually resolved well before a complaint crosses a court clerk's desk. Often, there is daylight between the precedent case and the new one. A cow becomes an iPad. Neighbors become strangers. A resource taken for convenience becomes one taken in an emergency.

When facts change, when the line from Case A to Case B is no longer straight and direct, then the analogy needs to contain both the specific facts from the precedent and a tie that shows the exact point of overlap between the two cases. To create this tie, a practitioner generalizes out from the specific details of the precedent and the specific details from the current case until the two fact sets overlap. For example, to make an analogy between a cow and an iPad, you could describe both as "things," but that describes a whole host of objects not relevant to the dispute. You could narrow the generalization by describing them as "possessions" of the farmer. Even more specifically, you could describe these objects as "business possessions" of the farmer, or items that help the farmer in his work. Finding the most specific way to connect the two ideas is key; to be overinclusive is to open your analogy up to devastating hypotheticals from your opponent. One scholar has called this finding the lowest common denominator between the facts of the two cases.[11]

The below example demonstrates the weakness of analogies without clear ties. This paragraph comes from a memo analyzing a potential false light claim against an artist who had publicly displayed a photo of an unconscious man with a bottle of whiskey at his kitchen table; his wife stares into the camera with a black eye. The photo was taken over a decade ago but was misdated as the current year. In the meantime, the man had recovered from his alcoholism and reunited with his wife, whom he no longer abused. The writer argues that this partial falsity is enough to satisfy the tort's requirement that the information presented be false:

> In *Jonap*, the falsity element was satisfied when an employer published a letter under an employee's name espousing both opinions the employee did hold and opinions he did not hold. Similarly, Fisher's photo showed Stall as currently an alcoholic and wife beater, when he had only been an alcoholic and abuser in the past.

That analogy places two sets of specific facts next to one another and leaves it to the reader to draw the connection between the two. The connection may be obvious to you, the writer, but it needs to be made concrete for the reader.

---

11. Paul T. Wangerin, *Skills Training in "Legal Analysis": A Systematic Approach*, 40 U. Miami L. Rev. 409, 451–52 (1986).

A more effective analogy finds the lowest common denominator between two sets of facts and uses that denominator to tie together the cases. In this example, the tie between these two cases is that, in both instances, part of the document that allegedly placed the plaintiff in a false light was true and part was false. The below analogy generalizes out from the specific facts to make that tie between the two cases explicit:

> While some of the letter attributed to the plaintiff in *Jonap* was true to his beliefs, other portions falsely characterized his beliefs. Similarly, Fisher's photograph simultaneously presented some truth about Tom Stall, while also falsely characterizing his activities.

Sandwiching this generalized tie between the specific facts of each case will create an effective case comparison, e.g.,

> A representation that is true in some respects, but untrue in others, qualifies as "false" for the purposes of the false light tort. In *Jonap*, the falsity element was satisfied when an employer published a letter under an employee's name espousing both opinions the employee did hold and opinions he did not hold. Although some of the letter was true to the plaintiffs' beliefs, other portions falsely characterized his beliefs. Similarly, Fisher's photograph simultaneously presents some truth about Tom Stall, while also falsely characterizing his activities. Fisher's photo showed Stall as currently an alcoholic and wife beater, when he had only been an alcoholic and abuser in the past.

A successful lowest common denominator will not only be specific enough to avoid overinclusivity, but it will also connect back to the legal rule or the policy underlying the rule. Many beginning law students draw a legal rule from a case, then construct an analogy to that case that does not apply the legal rule. For example, in our act-of-God contract case, a novice paragraph could look something like this:

> Nonperformance under a contract is excused when an Act of God occurs. An Act of God is a natural disaster that the plaintiff could not have foreseen and could have taken no action to prevent. *Bell*, 534 F.2d at 64. In *Bell*, the farmer was excused from performance because a flood destroyed his entire spinach harvest. This complete destruction was an act of God. Here, the farmer should also be excused from performance because his entire tomato harvest was destroyed.

This is not an effective analogy because it misses the point. The legal rule the writer is seeking to prove is not "complete destruction is an act of God."

Instead, it is "an act of God is a natural disaster the plaintiff could not have foreseen and could have taken no action to prevent." The facts relevant to foreseeability and prevention, and the lowest common denominator related to those facts, should have been the focus of the analogy. Compare that to the Jonap analogy above, where the lowest common denominator tied back to the "partial falsity" legal rule.

2. Distinctions

When crafting analogies, identifying the lowest common denominator provides a connection between the cases. Zooming out from the specific details allows you to find the similarity necessary to convince a reader that they are, in fact, analogous.

But when you instead want to distinguish a case, or show why the outcome under the current set of facts should be different than the outcome under a past case, you generally need to zoom in and show each case in crisp detail. By identifying these specific differences, you show how the lines of the cases do not touch.

An example of this zoom in/zoom out style can be found when comparing district court decisions in lawsuits against the NSA's metadata collection program. Judge William Pauley found that the program did not violate the Fourth Amendment and rested his analysis on an analogy to *Smith v. Maryland*,[12] a Supreme Court case that held using a pen register, which collected and recorded the telephone numbers dialed from the defendant's home, did not violate the Fourth Amendment because the caller did not have a reasonable expectation of privacy in that information. The connection between the two cases—the zoom out—was that an individual "has no legitimate expectation of privacy in information provided to third parties."[13] Because the telephone numbers in *Smith* were provided to the phone company, and the information in *ACLU* was provided to the phone company, callers had no expectation of privacy in that information.[14]

But in a different case, on nearly identical facts, Judge Richard Leon found that these two cases were distinct, and the NSA did violate the Fourth Amend-

---

12. 442 U.S. 735, 745–46 (1979).

13. Am. Civil Liberties Union v. Clapper, 959 F. Supp. 2d 724, 749, 752 (S.D.N.Y. 2013) (internal citation omitted), *aff'd in part, vacated in part, remanded*, 785 F.3d 787 (2d Cir. 2015).

14. *Smith*, 442 U.S. 735, 744–45.

ment through its bulk collection program.[15] He did so by focusing on the specific details of the cases, rather than the generalized "communication to third parties" highlighted by Judge Pauley. He conceded that the types of information at issue—phone numbers dialed, dates, times, and length of call—was limited, as was the information in Smith.[16] But the ubiquity of phones and, more specifically, mobile phones, "has dramatically altered the quantity of information that is now available and, more importantly, what that information can tell the Government about people's lives."[17] He went on to catalogue the various ways in which individuals' relationships to their phones had changed over the thirty-four years since *Smith* had been decided.[18]

Thus, by focusing on the specific facts of *Smith* (one landline telephone, a targeted investigation) and the specifics of the current case (almost every cellphone and landline in the United States, a bulk collection) Judge Leon crafted a distinction that showed why the rule of *Smith* should not apply to the NSA program. As he stated, "[T]he Smith pen register and the ongoing NSA Bulk Telephony Metadata Program have so many significant distinctions between them that I cannot possibly navigate these uncharted Fourth Amendment waters using as my North Star a case that predates the rise of cell phones."[19]

---

15. *Klayman v. Obama*, 957 F. Supp. 2d 1, 42 (D.D.C. 2013), *vacated and remanded*, 800 F.3d 559 (D.C. Cir. 2015).

16. *Id.* at 35.

17. *Id.* at 36.

18. *Id.*

19. *Id.* at 37.

Unit 2

Communicating Legal Reasoning

The first half of this text introduced the intricacies of legal reasoning. The second half will explore how to communicate that reasoning to judges, colleagues, clients, or others.

The dichotomy of this book may imply a schism between legal reasoning and communication of that reasoning, between internal deliberation and external messaging. But nothing could be further from the truth. Reasoning does not end once writing begins; the act of writing down thoughts clarifies and strengthens ideas, and may even lead to new ideas.

Communication is the second phase of the reasoning process, the X-ray machine that closely examines ideas, exposing minute cracks in the reasoning skeleton. Sometimes, the lawyer can set the broken bones. In other cases, the wounds run too deep and the lawyer must amputate the argument. It is only through the process of writing ideas down that a lawyer can determine which category the argument falls into.

The lawyer's task is thus to impose writing order on reasoning chaos. But to effectively do so, an attorney must know how to best respond to a given situation. The contours of a document—its tone, its goal, its content—vary depending on the *rhetorical situation.*

The rhetorical situation is made up of three elements: the exigence (i.e., the thing waiting to be done), the audience (i.e., those who are reading the piece and have the ability to make decisions or effect change), and the constraints (i.e., the things that have the power to constrain action).[1] Before drafting any legal document, first assess these three factors. Then, tailor your document to best respond to these factors.

---

1. Lloyd F. Blitzer, *The Rhetorical Situation*, 1 PHIL & RHETORIC 1, 6 (1968).

For an attorney drafting a legal document, the *exigence* is the situation that gives rise to the need for the document. Let's say a client comes to you after she has bought a house that, unbeknownst to her, was infested with mold in the basement. That exigence gives rise to a need for legal advice. The document will respond to that exigence by neutrally assessing risk, weighing the pros and cons of proceeding with a litigation, and providing sufficient information to enable the partner to provide thorough and thoughtful counsel to the client. A document that takes the side of the client and presents only those arguments favorable to the client would not be an appropriate response to this exigence because it would not adequately arm the reader with sufficient information to make a decision or take action.

The *audience* for your document is the primary reader of the material. In our moldy house example, the audience may be either another lawyer or a client (or perhaps both). Assuming that the primary audience is an attorney, the document can make assumptions about the legal knowledge of the reader and leave certain baseline presumptions unsaid. For example, one lawyer would not need to say to another, "The first decision on the merits of a case is usually a motion to dismiss, followed by a motion for summary judgment." Instead, the lawyer-writer can simply assess the client's likelihood of success at each stage. But these assumptions would be inappropriate in a document intended for a layman audience. An effective document in those circumstances might take a more plain-language approach, and may have to explain the assumptions that were silent in a lawyer-to-lawyer document.

The *constraints* on the document are the limits on the ways you can answer the legal question. These constraints can include (a) the exact contours of the legal question asked; (b) the procedural rules governing the case; and (c) prior precedent, which would constrain a judge deciding a case. In a memo, for example, the specific question posed limits the zone of relevant answers. The attorney writing a memo on whether the client could sue for fraud over the mold in her house should not address whether she could also sue for intentional infliction of emotional distress.

Procedural rules can also play an important constraining role. For example, the summary judgment standard requires "no genuine issue of material fact." Thus, if you were arguing that summary judgment should be granted, an argument that your opponent is wrong on a material fact would not prevail. The procedural constraints instead require that you argue that there is no factual dispute, and you win on the law.

Precedent plays perhaps the most constraining role in any kind of legal document. As discussed in Chapter 1, a court may be bound by a multitude of legal authorities, including statutes, regulations, or decisions issued by courts that sit higher in the hierarchy of authority. These decisions constrain what a court may do. For example, even if a judge strongly disagrees with binding precedent, even if she believes it was wrongly decided, she must follow it.

The components of the rhetorical situation are thus the first step in determining the contours for an effective document responding to that situation. The sections to follow provide some suggestions for how to effectively respond to the rhetorical situation in various legal writing contexts.

Chapter 7

Organizing Legal Reasoning

If you were to ask an attorney to list the key features of good legal writing, chances are "well-organized" would be near the top. This chapter explains why and offers guidance in meeting professional expectations.

Preliminarily, although organization may vary according to a specific document's exigence and audience (Is it an informal email to a supervisor? A formal memorandum? A brief to a court?), most legal documents contain the following sections, in roughly this order. The rhetorical situation of the document you are writing determines the level of detail you provide within each section.

1. **Introduction.** Because research is performed for a purpose (like advising a client, making a strategy decision, or persuading a court), readers expect to learn the outcome—what will or *should* happen—immediately. Reiterating the legal issue reminds the supervisor of the question posed and offers context to a subsequent reader, who may be less familiar with the case. In a brief, these features persuasively frame the legal issue at the outset, steering the court toward the ruling sought.

2. **Background.** An attorney analyzes law in relation to a particular set of circumstances. In a narrow research memo, the relevant facts might consist of a sentence. In a formal memo or brief submitted to a court, a complete narrative of the relevant facts usually precedes the legal arguments.

3. **Analysis or Argument.** This is the heart of the document, explaining how the conclusion stated at the outset is supported—or required—by law. If the writing is an office memo, legal analysis typically appears in the "Discussion" section; for a brief, legal analysis typically appears in the "Argument" section.

4. **Conclusion.** When an analysis is lengthy, it may be useful to sum up the key points at the end. If the writing is an office memo or email, this sum-

mary might include a recommendation or offer to engage in additional research. For a brief, always check the court rules for specific rules of form; courts take these seriously, which means you should, too.

These sections form the large-scale outline of your document. But organization must take place within each section as well. In this chapter, we focus on the organization of legal analysis or argument. The chapters ahead on objective and persuasive writing provide organizational tips for the other sections.

Organization is paramount because, as you've seen in the previous chapters, legal reasoning quickly becomes complex. But for an audience to be able to use the reasoning you have presented to make a decision, she must understand that reasoning, and understand it quickly. In the typical scenario, the author is intimately familiar with the relevant law and facts, but the reader is not. This means the reader will be unable to fill in unstated information or recognize implicit connections between ideas (especially if pressed for time). Steven Pinker has identified an author's inability to conjure the reading experience of a less informed audience as a primary cause of ineffective, unclear writing; he calls this phenomenon the "curse of knowledge."[1] Organized, structured analysis helps bridge that gap, by ensuring the necessary pieces are present and the more abstract connections are clearly visible.

Strong organization builds that bridge by achieving three different goals. The first is facilitative. Legal documents are used to make decisions, whether advising a client or urging a favorable ruling on a motion. Because the writer is usually not present when the reading occurs, sound organization helps ensure the writer's intended points are accurately conveyed to the reader.

The second is functional. A memo or brief is not necessarily read cover to cover, front to back, but consulted, piecemeal. A typical legal reader has a heavy caseload, with disparate matters demanding responses and decisions. Explicit organization helps the reader easily locate the relevant issue as needed.

The third is substantive. Effective organization in legal writing tracks and reinforces strong reasoning. Ideally, the logic and organization of a written analysis are fully integrated. When organization founders, even brilliant reasoning will be perceived as disarrayed thought, undermining the author's conclusions and credibility.

Now we'll look at how to organize legal analysis, addressing both "large-scale organization" and "small-scale organization."

---

1. Stephen Pinker, The Sense of Style: The Thinking Person's Guide to Writing in the 21st Century 59 (2014) ("Call it the Curse of Knowledge: a difficulty imagining what it is like for someone else not to know something that you know.").

A. Large-Scale Organization

Think of your legal document as a building. The large-scale organization of that document is the framework, the structure that houses and supports your individual units of analysis. To effectively build this frame, you need to carefully plan out how your main construction materials—here, your conclusions and legal rules—will fit together to create a sturdy support. We walk through each stage of that construction below.

1. Multiple Issues

The first step in large-scale organization is determining how many floors your building will have. Is this a single-issue analysis, or are there multiple issues? An issue is the general legal claim at stake, such as defamation or a violation of the Copyright Act. More than one issue will often arise from the same set of facts. For example, a photographer might claim that an art gallery physically altered her self-portrait by mishandling it and also defamed her by exhibiting the altered work under her name. The photographer might bring an action under an art preservation statute for the alteration of the artwork and a defamation claim for the alleged misrepresentation. These two issues are separate causes of action with distinct rules yet are derived from the same circumstances and thus alleged in a single complaint.

When a legal problem contains multiple discrete issues, as in our example above, each issue must be analyzed separately. A memo written to assess our hypothetical example could be structured like this:

I. Art Preservation
   [Analysis of art preservation issue]

II. Defamation
   [Analysis of defamation issue]

Separating out and clearly labeling each analysis is an effective strategy when the analysis under each issue is lengthy or complex. The legal reader—whether a supervisor or judge—is typically pressed for time and juggling multiple cases. Although the content of the analysis should identify each issue, headings allow the reader to quickly find them. But headings may not be necessary in something like an email that devotes a single paragraph to each issue. The key here is to ensure that you are analyzing these issues *separately*; conflating them is a quick route to confusion.

Relatedly, where you have more than one legal issue, consider beginning your analysis with a roadmap paragraph that lays out the different issues you plan to address. For the hypothetical art preservation/defamation memo, the roadmap could look something like this:

> The plaintiff can argue (1) that the defendant violated the art preservation statute, and (2) that the defendant defamed her. However, neither claim is likely to succeed.

This kind of paragraph is useful, especially for complex documents with multiple moving parts, as it provides readers with a map for the analysis to come. Orienting readers in this way primes them to more quickly understand the structure of the analysis and enables them to jump right to the part of the analysis that they are most interested in, thus saving time.

2. Components of Each Issue

Now we'll look at organizing the analysis within a single issue. In Chapter 4(A), you learned how to break down a rule into its component parts. That deconstructed rule is the starting point for organizing the analysis of each issue. The first step is deciding how many units should be constructed, and the second step is arranging them effectively, so they logically relate to one another.

Let's walk through the process, using a rule comprised of elements. Assume an artist can bring suit against (1) another "person" who (2) "intentionally commit[s]," (3) "any physical defacement, mutilation, alteration, or destruction," of (4) the artist's work of "fine art." Just as each legal issue should be analyzed separately, each element requires a discrete analysis.

As with a multi-issue analysis, your analysis of a multi-component rule should begin with a "roadmap" paragraph. This roadmap articulates the governing rule, with a citation to its source of authority, previewing its components in a logical order for discussion (which will often track the order in which the elements are presented in the original rule but need not, as with our example below). Here is an example of a roadmap paragraph in an office memo:

> To prove the statute was violated, an artist must establish (1) a work of "fine art," was subject to (2) "physical defacement, mutilation, alteration, or destruction," (3) "intentionally commit[ted]," (4) by another "person." Mass. Gen. Laws ch. 231, §85S (c). In the present case, Blair is an individual, and thus indisputably a "person." Diaz should have no trouble showing that her chair-sculpture qualifies as a work

of "fine art," and that Blair likely moved her sculpture "intentionally." However, Diaz's claim is unlikely to succeed because moving a sculpture from one room to another is not a "physical defacement, mutilation, alteration, or destruction" of the work.

A word of warning: Although a brief explanation of your conclusion on each element may be helpful, as occurs above, the roadmap should be concise. Too much detail up front—whether in the form of facts or how the law works—will prove just as confusing to readers as no roadmap at all. Consider, too, whether the conclusions are necessary in a roadmap; some readers prefer this model, while others simply want the breakdown of the rule into its component parts. Looking at past models of legal documents prepared for your reader will help you to decide whether to include the level of detail exemplified above in your own roadmap.

As mentioned, the components of a rule must also be arranged so that their relationship to one another is apparent. Are the components elements, each of which must be satisfied (as in the example above)? Or are they factors that must be aggregated at the end? Does a totality of the circumstances analysis govern? If so, what factors will be addressed in the analysis?[2] The roadmap presents readers with your "floor plan," ensuring both easy navigation to the desired part of the analysis and an understanding of how the parts fit together.

Just because a rule contains several components presenting potential or required means of triggering the rule, however, does not mean each component must be analyzed in your writing. Rather, your written analysis would be governed by the rhetorical situation: there may be constraints imposed by the assignment, strategy, procedural context, or facts. In other words, why build a large, multi-unit space with adjoining doors when the interested party merely seeks a small studio? Perhaps your supervisor has limited the analysis to one element preliminarily, because she thinks it's the most likely foundation for a motion to dismiss. Or a rule may be satisfied in three different ways, but one is patently inapplicable to the facts or too obviously satisfied to warrant discussion (e.g., a statute requires the plaintiff to be a living person and Martha, the plaintiff, is alive). Advise readers of these constraints up front to avoid misunderstandings, as in the following example:

> To prove the statute was violated, an artist must establish (1) a work of "fine art," was subject to (2) "physical defacement, mutilation, alteration, or destruction," (3) "intentionally commit[ted]," (4) by an-

---

2. Note that in a litigation context, even when both sides are applying the same rule, your breakdown may differ from that of your adversary.

other "person." Mass. Gen. Laws ch. 231, § 85S (c). This analysis is limited to element (2), whether any physical defacement, mutilation, alteration or destruction occurred.

As a practice point, you should identify particular limitations in a written analysis submitted to a supervisor even when the supervisor imposed the limitations.

After stating a roadmap paragraph, address each component of the rule in turn, mirroring the order presented in the roadmap. Just as with multiple claims, headings can be a useful way to delineate the various components, for example:

I. <u>Art Preservation Statute</u>
   [roadmap paragraph]

   1. <u>Work of Fine Art</u>
     [analysis]

   2. <u>Act of Physical Alteration</u>
     [analysis]

   3. <u>Intentionally Committed</u>
     [analysis]

The analysis of a single element or factor may require yet another tier of sub-divisions. Suppose that "fine art" is defined in the statute, which then becomes the main rule governing the sub-section addressing the work of fine art element:

"Fine art" means any original work of visual or graphic art of any media which shall include any painting, print, drawing, sculpture, or photograph, or any combination thereof, of recognized quality.[3]

The object at issue in Diaz's case looks like a chair, but she insists it is a sculpture. Your research finds case law involving items that courts have accepted as "sculpture" and, separately, what constitutes "recognized quality." Your written analysis would have two sub-elements under the "fine art" element: (a) "sculpture" and (b) "recognized quality." Because you would now have a two-part analysis, the structure should be previewed with a mini-roadmap, an example of which is illustrated below:

The statute defines "fine art" as "any original work of visual or graphic art of any media which shall include any painting, print, drawing,

---

3. This definition is hypothetical.

sculpture, or photograph, or any combination thereof, of recognized quality." *Id.* Here, the object likely (a) constitutes a "sculpture," and (b) is of "recognized quality."

The overall structure would be expanded as follows:

I. Art Preservation Statute
   [roadmap paragraph]

   1. Work of Fine Art
      [mini-roadmap]

      (a) Original Work of Sculpture
          [analysis]

      (b) Recognized Quality
          [analysis]

   2. Act of Physical Alteration
      [analysis]

   3. Intentionally Committed
      [analysis]

The basic principle to follow when thinking about your large-scale structure is organizing around the rules of law—not around individual cases, facts, or counterarguments. There are exceptions, but unless you have reason to deviate, this path should be your default.

B. Small-Scale Organization

Once you have established the floor plan, you need to design each individual unit. "Small-scale organization" refers to the organization of your writing within each section and sub-section, and it plays a pivotal role in constructing strong legal analysis.

Small-scale organization emulates the logical paradigm of deductive reasoning: the rule, like the major premise in a syllogism, must be placed up front. Let's look at an example. The following excerpt from a formal memo analyzes the "attack" element in a statute imposing owner liability for dog bites:

> Beatrice did not "attack" Fleck. *See* Minn. Stat. § 347.22. Attack means to move against with more or less violent intent. *Lewellin ex rel. Heirs of Lewellin v. Huber*, 465 N.W.2d 62, 64 (Minn. 1991) (quoting Webster's Third New Int'l Dictionary 140 (1971)). In *Lewellin*, the court

found no attack where a dog distracted a car driver when it jumped in the front seat to retrieve its toy. The driver lost control of the car and fatally struck a child, and the court reasoned that the dog had not moved with violent intent. *See id.* Beatrice similarly had no violent intent. She jumped up to see over the fence, which had the side effect of distracting Fleck and causing her fall from the ladder. Therefore, Beatrice did not attack Fleck within the plain meaning of the term.

This paragraph can be distilled into the following syllogism, a sign that organization is successfully fused with reasoning:

A dog only "attacks" if it moves against a person with some "violent intent." (major premise)
Beatrice did not move against Fleck with any violent intent. (minor premise)
Therefore, Beatrice did not attack Fleck. (conclusion)

You may have heard any number of acronyms referenced when professors, lawyers, or law students discuss organization and legal writing, e.g., IRAC, TREAC, CREAC, CRuPAC, CRAC. The commonalities between these structures are R, A, and C, which map directly on to a syllogism. The "R" is always the rule (the major premise). The "A" is the application of the rule to your client's facts (the minor premise). And the "C" is the conclusion that results from the combination of the major premise and the minor premise.

The additional letters in the acronyms largely assist in communicating the syllogism to your audience. Thus, prior to stating the rule up front, an introductory sentence may present the issue analyzed ("I"), topic ("T"), or your conclusion for that segment of the analysis ("C"). The rule ("R") is stated and then followed by a proof or explanation of the rule ("P" or "E"), which is the explanation of how the rule has been applied through your precedents. Application of the rule (the "A") usually occurs through analogies and distinctions with the facts of your case. In this respect, analogical reasoning operates within the deductive paradigm, helping to persuade the audience of the conclusion's validity.[4] Whichever acronym you choose, remember that its core is the major premise/minor premise/conclusion structure of the syllogism.

This example contains a simple analysis. But as discussed in the deductive reasoning chapter, syllogisms are often complex, heightening the need for wise

---

4. *See* Kristen Konrad Tiscione, Rhetoric for Legal Writers: The Theory and Practice of Analysis and Persuasion 104 (2d ed. 2016) (noting that analogies do not offer conclusive reasoning but have significant persuasive power within deductive reasoning).

choices and skilled craftsmanship. For example, there is no restriction on how much rule explanation is required in a given case. The degree depends upon the rule and facts, with greater ambiguity requiring more explanation than a rule narrowly-tailored to your facts. How much text should be devoted to applying the rule to the facts (your analogies and distinctions) will likewise vary.

This organizational structure is used in persuasive writing as well. Let's examine a few short excerpts from an appellate brief containing a procedural argument in a class action lawsuit against Google.[5] Google, the appellant, contended that the lower court had incorrectly certified the class under Rule 23 of the Federal Rules of Civil procedure.[6]

Here is the first sentence of each paragraph of this argument, along with the rule statement pertaining to Rule 23's "adequacy" requirement (all citations have been omitted). You should be able to see the elements of small-scale organization introduced by each sentence despite the missing text:

- Rule 23(a)'s "adequacy" requirement precludes certifying a class in these circumstances.

- It is axiomatic that a putative representative cannot adequately protect the class if the representative's interests are antagonistic to or in conflict with the objectives of those being represented. [] Under this rule, a class cannot be certified where class representatives "claim to have been harmed by the same conduct that benefitted other members...."

- Courts have denied class certification where the class representatives' objectives are fundamentally at odds with a significant portion of the proposed class.

- A similar clash of interests precludes certifying a class here.

- The district court erred as a matter of law in failing to give any weight to this evidence of a fundamental conflict in the class.

Remember that these sentences have been extracted from multiple paragraphs. In a simple analysis, your small-scale organization may consist of a single paragraph, as with the dog bite analysis. Or it may extend to multiple paragraphs, as occurs in the Rule 23 analysis partially reproduced here.

---

5. For the complete argument, see Brief for Appellant, Authors Guild v. Google Inc., 721 F.3d 132 (2d Cir. 2013) (No. 12-3200-cv), 2012 WL 5817270, at *17–21.

6. FED. R. CIV. P. 23.

Chapter 8

Legal Documents

A legal document generally aims to either inform or persuade, depending on the rhetorical situation. An objective analysis takes no sides ahead of time; it informs the reader of the attorney's neutral assessment of the law and the facts. Our advice to a client on her mold-in-the-basement problem would fall within this category. A persuasive argument has a pre-set outcome it aims to achieve; it is an analysis of the law through the lens of that outcome. A motion filed in a lawsuit against the previous owner who failed to disclose the mold problem would be a persuasive document.

The sections below provide advice for effectively communicating in each of these modes, but, regardless of whether you aim to inform or persuade, the basic structure of communicating legal analysis remains the same.

As we noted in the chapter on organization, legal communications can be distilled into four basic sections: Introduction, Background, Analysis (for objective documents) or Argument (for persuasive ones), and Conclusion. The length of each of these sections varies considerably depending on the kind of document. An introduction in an email is considerably shorter than one in a memo; a conclusion in a brief is often a single line, whereas one in a memo may be paragraphs long. The lessons below provide guidelines for each of these sections in different contexts—objective or persuasive writing—but always keep in mind the ultimate goal of these documents. Where departing from the techniques below better achieves the goal of informing or persuading the reader, then depart.

A. Objective Writing: Memos

One common form of objective writing is the office memo. Often, before filing a litigation (or during a litigation) attorneys will seek to provide advice to a client or neutrally analyze a relevant legal issue. The vehicle for communicating these predictions and analyses is often a memo from lawyer to lawyer or lawyer to client.

A memo accomplishes two goals simultaneously: (1) it helps the writer to think through the problem, and (2) it communicates the legal analysis and conclusion to others, either attorneys or client. The first task relies on many of the legal reasoning skills outlined in earlier chapters, but here is where the rubber meets the road. As the thinking and writing processes are deeply intertwined, an attorney must use the writing of the memo as an opportunity to clarify her thinking about an issue. Challenges that were hidden when the ideas were amorphous become concrete once they are committed to paper. Think of the draft of the memo as the lawyer's beta test. It is where any reasoning missteps are uncovered and corrected.[1]

A different challenge arises when an attorney attempts to convey her well-reasoned conclusions to other individuals. The thinking through of a legal problem is largely a messy internal dialogue. To successfully communicate that thinking to others, the lawyer must craft a memo that encourages readers to engage with and comprehend the material on the page. She must know how to effectively organize at the large and small scales, provide sufficient context to elicit understanding of the material, and guide the reader step-by-step through her analysis.[2] The memo thus must not only be well-reasoned and objective, but it must also clearly convey its conclusions so that they are comprehensible to those standing outside the lawyer's mind.

The sections below provide specific techniques to accomplish both of these goals.

1. Introduction: Question Presented/Brief Answer

With any introduction to an objective document, a reader needs to know both what the writing is about (the topic) and what the writer is trying to accomplish (the point). Failing to provide one or the other piece of information at the beginning of a document leaves a reader deeply confused from the start.

Identifying the *topic* early on enables the reader to comprehend and retain the material much more efficiently than by simply jumping into the weeds of

---

1. *See* Kirsten K. Davis, *"The Reports of My Death Are Greatly Exaggerated": Reading and Writing Objective Legal Memoranda in a Mobile Computing Age*, 92 Or. L. Rev. 471, 489 (2013).

2. *See id.* at 515–17.

a discussion.[3] Read through the following paragraph, which is missing a clear topic. Does it make any sense?

> The procedure is actually quite simple. First you arrange things into different groups depending on their makeup. One pile may be sufficient, depending upon how much there is to do. Then you put the items into a machine along with water and a chemical solution. Turn on the machine and wait for it to complete. Remove the items.[4]

It is very difficult to know exactly what the author here is taking about. But recipients of a similar paragraph were told in advance that the passage was about washing clothes. Participants who read just the paragraph could barely remember it, but the level of comprehension and recall almost doubled among participants who were told the topic of the passage.[5] The lesson: a reader must know the topic of a text to be able to understand and retain it.

The *point* of the writing is an equally crucial piece of information. As Stephen Pinker wrote, "Human behavior in general is understandable only once you know the actor's goals. When you see someone waving her arms, the first thing you want to know is whether she is trying to attract attention, shoo away flies, or exercise her deltoids."[6] Clearly stating the point of a piece of writing near the beginning gives the reader a lens through which to view everything that follows. That lens enables a crisp and clear picture of the information to come.

Your introduction thus must give the reader both the topic and the point of your document. With memos, the topic is usually the legal question posed, and the point is the answer to that question. An introduction can provide that information in a number of ways, such as through an executive summary or an abstract, but one common approach in memo-writing is the Question Presented/Brief Answer combination.

In this format, the Question Presented provides crucial information about the problem posed: the jurisdiction, legal question, and key facts. The jurisdiction is crucial because your reader wants to know what legal authorities are

---

3. *See, e.g.*, Stephen Pinker, The Sense of Style: The Thinking Person's Guide to Writing in the 21st Century 147 (2014); John D. Bransford & Marcia K. Johnson, *Contextual Prerequisites for Understanding: Some Investigations of Comprehension and Recall*, 11 J. Verbal Learning & Verbal Behav. 717, 720 (1972).

4. This example is based loosely off of one that appeared in Bransford & Johnson, *supra* note 3, at 722.

5. *Id.* at 723.

6. Pinker, *supra* note 3, at 148.

binding on a court deciding this issue. The legal question lays out the general topic, and the key facts provide the context of how this legal question arose.

For example:

> Under Connecticut common law, did photographer Claire Fisher place her subject Tom Stall in a false light when she displayed a misdated photograph of him that suggested he is currently an alcoholic and domestic abuser?

Here, the phrase "Connecticut common law" provides the jurisdiction, "place her subject in a false light" raises the legal question, and "when she displayed ..." are the key facts of the case. One way to ensure all these pieces are included is to structure your Question Presented as "Under [jurisdiction], did [legal question] when [key facts]?"

The Brief Answer solves the question by supplying a short answer (yes, no, probably yes, maybe no, etc.), followed by the relevant legal conclusions that support that short answer. You should also provide here any key facts supporting those legal conclusions not already mentioned in the Question Presented. Here's an example of a Brief Answer responding to the Question Presented above:

> Probably yes. While Stall had abused both alcohol and his wife in the past, he had been sober and non-abusive for ten years. A depiction of him as currently a wife abuser is both false and would be highly offensive to a reasonable person. Fisher acted with reckless disregard because she had been notified by an assistant that the date associated with the photograph was likely false, but she did not recheck it. She also posted the photo in public view, as it was displayed in the waiting room of a domestic violence shelter, a space that was open to the public.

From this Brief Answer, the reader knows that all four elements of a false light invasion of privacy claim are met. The key fact supporting the conclusion that each element is met is also included: The picture is false because it paints Stall as a domestic abuser, which he is not. That accusation would be highly offensive to a reasonable person. Fisher did not double-check the date, which is evidence of reckless disregard. The photo could also be seen by anyone who stopped into the domestic violence clinic, which supports a conclusion that it was in public view.

However, if the writer concluded that the defendant did not place the plaintiff in a false light, the Brief Answer could read something like this:

> No. Stall will fail to prove that the exhibit was displayed in public view or was substantially certain to become public knowledge. Only ten peo-

ple had seen the exhibit since it opened and more visits in the future are unlikely, as the show did not receive any publicity or advertising.

That Brief Answer provides a short answer—"no"—along with the legal conclusion on the element of the false light claim that is not met: the public view element. This legal conclusion is effective because it provides a reader with the critical fact on which the conclusion turns, the fact that only ten people had seen the exhibit and a future uptick in attendance was unlikely.

Novice legal writers run into the same problems with introductions—and especially with Question Presented/Brief Answer structures—again and again. The first common mistake is to fail to provide enough information to support the legal conclusion. For instance, it would not be enough for a Brief Answer to conclude: "No, Fisher did not place Stall in a false light." This general statement does not provide enough detail for a reader to understand the point, i.e., the solution to the legal problem. Without diving deeper and supplying the conclusion on the specific elements that drive the answer to the legal question, the memo would remain rudderless until the analysis section.

A second common mistake is to avoid any concrete answer to the legal question. The memo's point is to solve a problem. To simply note that "the judge will have to decide" is not helpful to a client looking to you for advice and guidance. The conclusion you have reached might not be airtight, but you must come down on one side or the other and explain the weaknesses of your argument (and why they do not control the outcome) in your analysis.

Common mistake number three: attempting to include too much information. Restrict the key facts presented in an introduction to the crucial facts of the case, i.e., the facts upon which the elements turn. Irrelevant facts should be pared away to avoid distracting the reader. In a Brief Answer like the one below, the key facts are lost in a sea of irrelevance:

No. Fisher did not place Stall in a false light because the photos were not accessible to the general public. The domestic violence clinic is located on a side street in the center of town. It has about 20 to 30 visitors a day, but few of those visitors walk into the side room where the exhibit is located. Only ten people have seen the exhibit in the last four weeks. Fisher plans to take down the exhibit in a month, although she is in conversations with the manager of the domestic violence clinic to extend the viewing period for an additional week. The show has received no advertising or publicity. No members of the Little League Baseball team coached by Stall have seen the exhibit.

Some of these facts provide additional support for the idea that the exhibit was not accessible to the public, but the overall effect is one of a deluge of facts. A more effective Brief Answer is pared to the essentials: the number of people who have seen the exhibit so far, and the likelihood that more will see it in the future. Other supportive facts will be introduced later to provide further support for your conclusions, but the introduction is not the place to introduce those facts. Restrict the introduction to the crucial fact or two that convinced you that this element will fall in your favor.

2. Background: Statement of Facts

After introducing the topic and the point of the memo, the next step is to provide the background necessary for your reader to understand the context of the case. At a minimum, this background should include the facts that govern the analysis.

The Statement of Facts section is critical, at least in part, because the factual circumstances of a case are constantly shifting. An analysis performed shortly after a client intake interview will be based wholly on the client's account of events. As factual investigation moves forward, through witness interviews, the discovery process, and other means, facts change, often significantly. This shifting ground could create cracks in the foundation of your analysis. A memo is thus a snapshot in time, and a future reader must know where the factual ground stood at the time the memo was written.

The goal here is to provide the legally relevant facts in an organized and comprehensible way. The challenge is twofold: (1) in a sea of facts, you must pick out the relevant ones, and (2) you must organize those facts into a cohesive narrative so the reader can easily understand them.

a. Legally Relevant Facts

How do you ensure that you have captured all the legally relevant facts? You must look to the legal authorities—statutes, cases, and other sources—for guidance. You may believe a fact is relevant, but the legal authorities could say otherwise.

For example, one of the elements under the false light invasion of privacy tort is that the information distributed must be false. Suppose the information peddled was that a married man was having an affair. You have several facts at your disposal indicating that the information is not false: the article is supported by a photograph showing the man and his supposed mistress kissing outside a hotel room, and the editor of the newspaper that printed the article insists that the story is true. But in the precedents, the truth of a statement has only been proven through documentary evidence, and courts have refused to rely on statements of newspaper employees vouching for the story. Thus, the only legally relevant fact is the photographic evidence of the affair.

Before looking to the cases, you may have thought that both of these facts provided some legally relevant information. After all, the fact that the editor stands behind his story may indicate to a layperson that the story is more true than false. But you only know what a court will take into account by looking at the facts that have driven past court decisions.

That said, if a court or legislature has not addressed whether a particular fact is relevant, but the fact tips the scales in one direction or another, then it should be included in your Statement of Facts. If no court had stated whether a newspaper employee's statements were relevant evidence in determining truth, then the fact that the editor stands behind the story could tip the scales in your client's direction and is information a reader of the memo would want to know.

One crucial point to keep in mind when selecting facts: negative facts are as legally relevant as positive facts. Facts that harm your client are as important—sometimes more important—as facts that support your client's position. You want to present those facts in your memo; to exclude them is to misinform your reader about the strength of your conclusion. Because the ultimate decision on what course of action to pursue rests with your client, she needs to be informed about the weaknesses in her position. This means including the negative facts in your Statement of Facts, as well as addressing those legally relevant negative facts in your analysis. We will discuss the importance of defusing counterarguments in our section on legal analysis.

One technique for ensuring that all the legally relevant facts are captured is to read through your analysis and highlight each fact you use in that section. Any fact used there—positive or negative—should be included in the Statement of Facts. For this reason, many attorneys draft a Statement of Facts after they have completed their analysis section. If you prefer to write the Statement of Facts first, run through it again after you have completed your analysis to ensure that all legally relevant facts have been captured.

b. Cohesive Narrative

Imagine a Statement of Facts strung together solely by legally significant facts. It would read something like this:

A photo that Claire Fisher took in 2006 and is currently on display in an area open to the public shows Tom Stall in the background of the photograph with an empty liquor bottle next to him. In the foreground is his wife, who has a black eye. The photograph is mislabeled with the date "2013," when it was actually taken in 2006. Fisher's assistant informed her that the date was inaccurate. About ten people saw the picture. Mr. Stall, who is no longer an alcoholic and does not currently beat his wife, was recently fired from coaching a youth baseball team after someone saw the picture and reported it to the league.

That's an adequate Statement of Facts because it presents the information the reader absolutely needs to know. But it is difficult to read because there is no narrative cohesion. The reader jumps from fact to fact without any linkage between the two.

Contextual facts create those links that make a Statement of Facts easy to read and understand:

> Claire Fisher, a professional photographer, recently installed a photography exhibit titled *Survivor* in the waiting room of the Lily Valley Women's Shelter in Bridgeport, Connecticut. Among the images depicting battered women was a picture of Edie Stall that Ms. Fisher had taken in 2006. At the time the photo was taken, Ms. Stall had been staying at the shelter after her husband, Tom Stall, punched her in the face in a drunken rage. Ms. Fisher took the photo in question while accompanying Ms. Stall to her home. It showed a bruised Ms. Stall in the foreground and Mr. Stall in the background, eyes closed, seated at the kitchen table with a nearly empty bottle of whiskey next to his hand.
>
> When the exhibit was assembled earlier this year, the placard accompanying the photograph bore the year 2013. Before the photos went on display, Ms. Fisher's assistant told her that the image had actually been taken in 2006. Ms. Fisher intended to double-check the dates but failed to do so. About ten people viewed the exhibit in the first two weeks it was open. Though the display was technically open to the public on a walk-in basis, the only patrons thus far have been shelter residents, staff, or registered visitors. It was not advertised anywhere and did not receive any press.
>
> One patron, Judy Danvers, recognized Mr. Stall as her son's coach in a local basketball league. Sam Carney, Mr. Stall's attorney, states that she successfully petitioned league officials to fire him. Mr. Carney reports that soon after the photograph was taken, Mr. Stall "vowed to turn his life around." He entered a rehabilitation clinic in late 2006 and has been sober since that time, and he reunited with Ms. Stall in

2008. Mr. Stall claims the photo paints him in a false light because it implies that he abused his wife in 2013.

Providing more context here helps the reader understand the nuances of the situation: that the photograph appeared in a women's shelter where a limited number of people have seen it; that Fisher intended to check the dates of the photograph but failed to do so; that Stall has turned his life around and is currently married to Ms. Stall. These contextual facts allow the reader to understand the challenges presented by the case. A jury may be sympathetic to Stall's story of redemption; it may also understand Fisher's human frailty in failing to check a minor detail. While not technically legally significant, they could nudge a decision-maker in one direction or the other. This kind of context provides valuable information to a reader, both because it makes the story of what happened clearer and easier to follow, and because it gives the reader some sense of the emotional peaks and valleys of this particular case.

A word of warning: Because the purpose of this memo is to predict an outcome, not advocate for an outcome, your Statement of Facts must be neutral and even-handed. There is a temptation when writing a factual narrative to gloss over the bad actions of a client or to overemphasize the facts helpful to your client's side. It is difficult to frame a story in a way that does not flatter the person who is paying your bills. Resist this tendency. Your client is better served by a clear-eyed recitation of the facts—one that makes the weaknesses in her position clear—than a flattering portrait. Flattering portraits mask landmines that can blow up litigation at a later stage. You do not want to give the client the impression all is well when the factual portrait the other side can paint will be devastating, either emotionally or legally.

3. Analysis: Discussion

The Discussion section is where you lay out, in minute detail, your legal analysis and conclusions. Use the principles of large-scale organization and small-scale organization discussed earlier. Some key reminders: Present a roadmap to begin your analysis. Organize your analysis around your breakdown of the main legal rule. Each separate section of the Discussion should front at least one (sometimes more than one) legal rule. When applying a legal rule through a factual analogy, be crisp and clear about the factual overlap between the cases.

The temptation here will be to constantly hedge your bets. In most cases that are on the cusp of litigation, there will be strong arguments on both sides, and there are no guarantees as to what a court presented with this case would do. All lawyers recognize this basic truth. The answer, then, is not to throw up your hands and say "I don't know what will happen." It is to reach a conclusion, make a prediction, but acknowledge the weaknesses of your own case. If there is a strong counter-argument to the conclusion you present, note it. Note, too, why you believe your conclusion stands despite the other side's strongest points.

There will also be a temptation to side with your client and argue persuasively on her behalf, but a strong Discussion section must remain neutral and even-handed. You are predicting an outcome, not advocating for a desired result. State legal rules as you expect the court would state them; do not try to frame them to favor your client, as you will do in your persuasive writing. Present the facts from precedent cases as they were discussed in those cases; do not re-frame them to suit your proposed narrative (another technique we will discuss in more depth in the section on brief-writing). An objective document's main goal is to neutrally present the information that helps the reader of the memo reach a decision; your tone should reflect that goal.

4. Conclusion

Just as with the other sections of the memo, the Conclusion section could be approached a number of different ways. Some readers prefer a short-and-sweet conclusion. Some prefer a lengthy executive summary section. Some don't want a Conclusion section at all. Looking at samples of past memos the reader found effective is the best way to ensure you are meeting her needs.

One common approach to Conclusions: provide a detailed summary of the overall conclusion you've reached, as well as your conclusion on each of the sub-topics you have analyzed. Your Question Presented and Brief Answer provide the most general conclusion (your answer on the overall question), while your main roadmap breaks down your analysis into its component parts. Your Conclusion can be more detailed than either of these sections; it can provide a breakdown of the elements, conclusions on each, and a conclusion on the overall legal question. Here's an example of how this could look:

> Stall's claim of false light invasion of privacy against Fisher will be unsuccessful because he can only prove three of the four required elements of the tort. Stall will fail to prove the publicity element because Fisher displayed the photo to only ten people, which is not enough qualify as a display in public or one that was substantially certain to become public knowledge. He will be able to prove that the photograph does meet the falsity element because the inaccurate

date is sufficient to make the entire display false. Additionally, the photograph would be considered highly offensive to a reasonable person because the portrayal that he is presently an alcoholic and abusive husband is a major misrepresentation of character. Finally, because Fisher had been warned that the date on the photograph was false yet failed to correct it, her actions will be seen as reckless disregard and satisfy the fourth element of the false light invasion of privacy tort.

B. Persuasive Writing: Briefs

With persuasive writing, our focus in this chapter, your goal shifts from neutrally informing an audience about a particular issue to convincing an audience to decide that issue in your favor. The destination is set. You must find the best road to it.

This shift in focus does not mean that you should discard the lessons learned from the previous chapters. Strong legal reasoning and clear communication of that reasoning remain the bedrocks of persuasive writing.

This truth is reflected in Aristotle's writings on rhetoric, which identified the pillars of persuasion as logos, ethos, and pathos.[7] Logos is the logic of the argument. All the legal reasoning methods discussed in Unit 1 relate to logos. Ethos is an appeal to the credibility of the speaker. As with objective writing, the clarity of your persuasive writing and its freedom from errors, stylistic or substantive, all boost your reputation.

Where persuasive and objective writing differ mainly rests with pathos. The effective advocate will not only convince her audience that she is correct through pure logic, but she will also stir the audience's emotions in favor of her client. Aristotle counseled that an audience who likes a man accused of a misdeed will have difficulty believing he acted wrongly, but an audience that dislikes that same man will take a dim view of his actions.[8] Modern rhetoricians and psychologists have investigated methods of eliciting those emotions. The

---

7. ARISTOTLE, THE BASIC WORKS OF ARISTOTLE 1329 (Richard McKeon ed., Random House 1941) ("Of the modes of persuasion furnished by the spoken word there are three kinds. The first kind depends on the personal character of the speaker [ethos]; the second on putting the audience into a certain frame of mind [pathos]; the third on the proof, or apparent proof, provided by the words of the speech itself [logos].").

8. *Id.* at 1379–80.

following sections introduce you to some of those insights and provide you with tools to incorporate pathos effectively in your own advocacy.

1. Legal Themes

One of the primary ways advocates harness the power of pathos-based argument is through an effective theme.[9] A theme taps into "shared values and civic virtues"[10] and assures the decision-maker that the outcome you desire is not only the logical result, it is also the right and just one. Oliver Wendell Holmes called these values his "can't helps," or the things that he can't help believing.[11] Judge Patricia Wald similarly acknowledged that, ideally, her "sense of ultimate rightness," along with the facts of the case and the logic of the arguments, would be the basis of her decision-making.[12]

That said, few advocates prevail on purely emotional appeals before a court of law. The backbone of any legal decision must be a logical one, grounded in the applicable legal rules. This logos counterpart to the pathos theme is typically called the legal theory. It is the rules-based reason why your side wins.

These two aspects of advocacy—theme and legal theory—form "a double helix of norms."[13] And just as base pairs bind to form a DNA double helix, so do themes and legal theories bind to create a cohesive, compelling reason for a ruling in your client's favor.

---

9. Much ink has been spilled identifying the non-legal connective tissue that unifies a brief. Some scholars use the term "theme"; others combine the ideas of a pathos-based justification and a logos-based justification into a single "theory of the case." *See, e.g.,* Steven Lubet, *Story Framing,* 74 TEMP. L. REV. 59, 59–60 (2001); RICHARD K. NEWMAN, JR. & KRISTEN KONRAD TISCIONE, LEGAL REASONING AND LEGAL WRITING 253–66 (7th ed. 2013). For simplicity's sake, we use "theme" to mean a pathos-based argument; we also separate out that idea from the logos-based argument for success, which we call the "legal theory."

10. Steven Lubet, *Story Framing,* 74 TEMP. L. REV. 59, 59 (2001).

11. OLIVER WENDELL HOLMES, THE ESSENTIAL HOLMES: SELECTIONS FROM THE SPEECHES, JUDICIAL OPINIONS, AND OTHER WRITINGS OF OLIVER WENDELL HOLMES, JR. 107 (Richard A. Posner, ed., Univ. of Chicago 1992) ("[W]hen I say that a thing is true, I only mean I can't help believing it—but I have no grounds for assuming that my can't helps are cosmic can't helps and some reasons for thinking otherwise. I therefore define the truth as the system of my intellectual limitations—there being a tacit reference to what I bet is or will be the prevailing can't help of the majority of that part of the world that I count.").

12. Patricia M. Wald, *The Rhetoric of Results and the Results of Rhetoric: Judicial Writings,* 62 U. CHI. L. REV. 1371, 1377 (1995).

13. Robert P. Burns, *Studying Evidence Law in the Context of Trial Practices,* 50 ST. LOUIS U. L.J. 1155, 1171 (2006).

So where do we look to uncover themes? Turn first to the values that a particular area of law aims to further. Contract law, for example, is founded in part on the idea that enforcing the reasonable expectations induced by a promise is a societal benefit.[14] A competing value in contract law is that parties should not be bound by promises they were deceived into making.[15] Thus, an advocate arguing that a contract should be enforced will evoke the instability caused by allowing a defendant to evade his commitments; the advocate arguing that the contract is invalid will point to the injustice inherent in binding an individual to the terms of a fraud.

Research Tip: Where can you find these values? Treatises are an excellent resource that often explain not only the black letter law in a particular area, but also the reasons why this black letter law came to pass. Some, but not all, treatises are available on the electronic databases; most treatises are available on either Lexis or Westlaw, but not necessarily on both platforms. Most law libraries have extensive collections of treatises for a host of subject areas. Reviewing more than one treatise for a particular subject area—both Corbin and Williston on Contracts, for example—helps you to understand the underlying values of this area of law. This is one research task that rewards spending the time looking at hard copies in a library.

If you have combed the legal literature of a specific doctrine and cannot find a solid thematic rock on which to build your case, expand your horizons. Themes based on commonly held legal norms, such as fairness and predictability, repeat themselves across the legal spectrum, regardless of the doctrinal

---

14. CORBIN ON CONTRACTS § 1.1 ("That portion of the field of law that is classified and described as the law of contracts attempts the realization of reasonable expectations that have been induced by the making of a promise. Doubtless, this is not the only purpose which motivated the creation of the law of contracts; but it is believed to be the main underlying purpose, and it is believed that an understanding of many of the existing rules and a determination of their effectiveness require a lively consciousness of this underlying purpose.").

15. WILLISTON ON CONTRACTS § 1.1 ("[A] contract enables parties to project exchange into the future and to tailor their affairs according to their individual needs and interests; once a contract is entered, the parties' rights and obligations are binding under the law, unless the contract is subject to some invalidating cause, such as fraud, mistake, duress, or the like, which would enable one of the parties to avoid its undertaking.").

area. In this way, legal themes mirror literary themes. Institutional dysfunction was a central theme of the HBO television show *The Wire*, which documented the impact of the police, courts, drug syndicates, schools, and media on individuals in Baltimore.[16] The same theme played out centuries earlier in the Greek tragedy *Antigone*, in which a king's unjust law led to the arrest and suicide of a woman who followed her moral principles instead of her sovereign's edicts.[17] These two dramas are separated by thousands of years and many cultural milieus, but their basic foundation is the same. And, as any English undergraduate who has scribbled "society vs. man" in a margin knows, it is a theme that has infused countless other works of literature.

Themes also recur in legal stories, regardless of whether the case is a breach of contract allegation, an invasion of privacy tort, or an issue of criminal procedure. The following is by no means an exhaustive list, but just a handful of common themes and excerpts from the briefs where they appear:

An eye for an eye. The only just result is for this individual/entity to pay for the harm he/she/it caused.

> Contrary to petitioner's contention, *her repeated use* of *highly toxic specialty chemicals* to *harm* Myrlinda Haynes was not for a "peaceful purpose." That commonsense proposition is confirmed by the statutory definition of the term, which is limited to socially productive, non-malicious activities.... Petitioner notes that the Act's prohibitions should extend only to conduct that, if undertaken by a State Party, would violate the Convention, but that observation does not assist her. A State Party's *malicious use* of a *toxic chemical* to *injure or kill* an individual is prohibited by the Convention,....[18]

---

16. *See generally* Kristin Henning, *"The Wire" Is Right About Everything: David Simon Nailed the Police, Media, Politicians*, Salon (June 14, 2015), http://www.salon.com/2015/06/14/the_wire_is_right_about_everything_david_simon_nailed_the_police_media_politicians/ ("With each year, the show's moral clarity and portrayal of rotted-out institutions/ambitious climbers stings more").

17. *See generally* Sophocles, Antigone, http://classics.mit.edu/Sophocles/antigone.html. David Simon, the creator of *The Wire*, has acknowledged the show's debt to Greek tragedies. "Those who want to know why Omar had to die, why Stringer had to die," he said, "Strap on a helmet, get in the game and read Antigone. Read Medea. It had to happen." Chris Barton, *"The Wire": David Simon Schools USC*, L.A. Times (Mar. 4, 2008), http://latimesblogs.latimes.com/showtracker/2008/03/the-wire-david.html.

18. Brief for the United States at 8–9, Bond v. United States, 134 S. Ct. 2077 (2014) (No. 12-158), 2013 WL 4407059 (emphases added).

The legal theory here is grounded in statutory interpretation, as the writer aims to prove that the defendant's acts do not fit within the statutory meaning of "peaceful purpose." That is one logos-based reason why the Respondent should prevail. But the advocate also peppers her argument with vibrant words that draw out the theme. Vivid language such as "highly toxic specialty chemicals," "repeated use," and "harm" crystallizes the damage done to the victim and creates a sense that this wrong must be righted.

A word of caution here: It is easy to go overboard when using the eye-for-an-eye theme, and judges and juries typically react poorly to bombast, wild claims, or unsupported characterizations of facts. The term "highly toxic specialty chemicals" is grounded in the facts of the case, as the defendant had placed two chemical compounds, one arsenic-based, the other used to print photographs, on the victim's doorknob. But characterizing those chemicals as, say, a "death trap" would have gone too far; the victim suffered only a minor chemical burn and both sides agreed the defendant did not intend to kill the victim. Opposing counsel could not quibble with "toxic chemicals," but if the writer had used the term "death trap," her opponent undoubtedly would have attacked her credibility and painted her as prone to exaggeration.

A second word of caution: This theme only works if it is tied to a valid legal argument. It usually does a plaintiff little good to spend paragraphs of her brief laying out a defendant corporation's past securities misdeeds if the relevant legal question is whether the corporation's internal documents are protected by the attorney-client privilege.[19] Simply because a theme is available does not mean it is the best theme for the particular case.

The consequences are dire. Adhering to the legal rule proposed by the other side will have abhorrent results.

> Rather than enforcing the prohibition on executing persons with mental retardation set out in *Atkins*, the Florida Supreme Court has redefined mental retardation so that it means something different — and narrower — than this Court's decision contemplated. Under Florida's rule, defendants who do not have an obtained IQ test score of 70 or below always fall outside *Atkins'* protections, regardless of the measurement error in all IQ tests. That is so even if — as here —

---

19. That said, if the defendant corporation had improperly used the attorney-client privilege in the past to shield securities misdeeds, then an eye-for-an-eye theme may be appropriate.

clinicians have uniformly diagnosed a defendant as having mental retardation....

The predictable consequence of Florida's rule is that persons with mental retardation will be executed. Without this Court's intervention, that will happen here. The evidence is overwhelming that Freddie Lee Hall has mental retardation. His teachers classified him as "mentally retarded" 60 years ago, and he has been diagnosed with mental retardation repeatedly over the course of several decades. Indeed, before *Atkins* was decided, the Florida courts agreed that Hall had been "mentally retarded his entire life...." *But Hall is now subject to execution because the Florida Supreme Court has decided that no defendant with an obtained IQ test score over 70 can have mental retardation.* That result cannot be squared with the Constitution.[20]

This theme works well when blind adherence to a legal rule leads to an egregious wrong. The more stringent and specific the rule, and the less flexibility it affords the judge, the more susceptible it is to this theme. An IQ score cut-off, for example, binds a decision-maker's hands, even when circumstances warrant deviating from that rule.

To successfully incorporate this theme, an advocate must point to a specific, horrific harm that would result from the rule. Generalities do not suffice. In the example above, the advocate pointed to detailed non-IQ evidence that Hall was mentally disabled—classifications of teachers, clinicians, and even the Florida courts themselves. Bald assertions that Hall was mentally disabled, devoid of that specific evidence, would not have as effectively persuaded the court that a dire result was imminent.

> **Don't trust 'em.** The other side is using the court as a means to achieve unjust ends.

> Petitioner was validly convicted of corruptly persuading its employees with the intent to cause them to withhold documents from, or alter documents for, an official proceeding, in violation of 18 U.S.C. 1512(b)(2)(A) and (B). *Petitioner portrays its document-destruction campaign, in the face of a looming SEC investigation, as wholly legitimate conduct ... as if American corporations routinely find it proper to instruct their employees to lay waste to vast troves of doc-*

---

20. Brief for Petitioner at 24–26, Hall v. Florida, 134 S. Ct. 1986 (2014) (No. 12-10882), 2013 WL 6673693 (emphases added).

uments when a government investigation is viewed as highly probable. Nothing could be further from the truth. Petitioner was not charged with having a document destruction policy as such. As the court of appeals recognized, "[t]here is nothing improper about following a document retention policy when there is no threat of an official investigation." ... *But when, after realizing that a government investigation is bearing down on it, a company seizes on a dormant or widely ignored document policy and uses it as a pretext to destroy evidence of its own or its client's potential misconduct, it is altogether another matter. No responsible entity would engage in such conduct; petitioner's own document policy prohibited it.* Petitioner's elaborate claims notwithstanding, its conduct represents a serious departure from well-established principles in the criminal law, and its conviction under Section 1512(b) should be affirmed.[21]

Here, the government suggests that the other side is not trustworthy and that their propositions are not to be believed. Notice how the government evokes a mismatch between what Arthur Andersen says and what the evidence (common practice and Arthur Andersen's own document policy) shows: that this was a situation where documents should have been retained, not destroyed.

Notice, too, what the advocate does not do: He does not wildly speculate, or call Arthur Andersen employees liars, or say that the conduct Arthur Andersen engaged in was beyond the pale. He marshals concrete evidence in support of that position. Those specific facts make this use of the theme so effective. Without the details, "don't trust 'em" themes can devolve into wild speculation and name-calling, which are rarely effective advocacy tools.

* * *

These, of course, are only a handful of examples. Many more themes can be found throughout the legal universe. To uncover them, consider not just the legal rules of the particular doctrine you are analyzing, but the values and norms that underlie those legal rules and the legal system as a whole. In those vast constellations of ideas live the themes that will streamline and unify your legal arguments.

Now that you have grappled with themes (in this section) and legal theories (in the chapters on legal reasoning), you are ready to learn how to intertwine

---

21. Brief for the United States at 14, Arthur Andersen LLP v. United States, 544 U.S. 696 (2005) (No. 04-368), 2005 WL 738080 (emphases added).

the two to create a powerful piece of written advocacy. The next section delves into how to express these central ideas.

2. Sections of a Brief

The theme and the legal theory should run through every part of your brief. They tie together the divergent sections and create a sense that a ruling in your client's favor is both legally correct and normatively sound.

Each section of the brief furthers that theme and legal theory in different ways. Some sections use the framing of the legal question to persuade. Others use storytelling devices, such as plot, setting, and character, to develop the theme. And still others lay out in meticulous detail the logical arguments that win the case. The chapters below identify the goals of each section of a typical brief and describe effective strategies for achieving those goals.

We use the brief as our example of written advocacy, but the four sections highlighted here—Introduction, Background, Argument (including Summary of Argument), and Conclusion—mirror those of any effective persuasive piece. When translating the techniques laid out below to non-brief contexts, keep those four requisites in mind. Testimony before Congress advocating for a legislative change will not have a formal Statement of the Issues Presented for Review, but, for the reasons highlighted below, it will be more persuasive if it introduces and frames the issue at the beginning of the testimony, just as an Issue Statement does.

Research Tip: The required contents of a brief vary by jurisdiction. Some courts mandate a summary of the argument,[22] others provide guidance as to what should be in that summary,[23] and still others do not require any summation of the argument at all[24] (although it is a good idea to include one unless the rules expressly prohibit it). The court rules of the jurisdiction provide instructions on what sections to include, formatting requirements, and submission formalities, among other critical pieces of information. Court rules include the rules for an entire type of court (e.g., the Federal Rules of Civil Procedure or the Federal Rules

---

22. *E.g.,* Fed. R. App. P. 28(a)(7).

23. *E.g.,* Sup. Ct. R. 24.1(h) (prohibiting the summary of the argument from merely repeating the pointheadings).

24. *Cf., e.g.,* Mass. R. App. P. 16(a)(4) (omitting the requirement of a summary of the argument from briefs whose argument section is shorter than twenty-five pages).

of Appellate Procedure); rules for a particular jurisdiction, also known as local rules (e.g., the Local Rules of the United States District Courts for the Southern and Eastern Districts of New York[25]); and, on occasion, rules for a particular judge's chambers, also known as individual rules (e.g., the Individual Rules and Procedures of the former S.D.N.Y. Judge Shira Scheindlin[26]). To ensure that the brief you are filing complies with these rules, you must examine all of them. For example, when filing a summary judgment motion before Judge Scheindlin, you would discover that a summary judgment motion must be filed within thirty days of the close of discovery;[27] that it must be accompanied by a short statement, in numbered paragraphs, of the undisputed material facts;[28] and that these fact statements must be limited to twenty-five pages.[29] Failure to adhere to any one of these requirements could result in a judgment adverse to your client. A search on Westlaw or Lexis is not sufficient to ensure that all this ground is covered; you must also consult the websites of the jurisdiction and the individual judge, which contain the most recent versions of local and individual rules.

---

a. Introduction: Question Presented, or Statement of the Issue Presented for Review

You learned in the chapter on objective writing that an introduction to a legal communication requires three key pieces of information: the legal question, your answer to the legal question, and the key facts supporting your answer. The same pieces of information must be included at the beginning of a persuasive document, but with two twists. First, when stating the legal question, ensure that you frame the question in the light most favorable to your side. You do not state the answer to the question outright, as in objective writing. You imply the answer through your shading of the question. Second, select and present facts in a way that is both indisputably accurate and persuasive.

---

25. BD. OF JUDGES OF THE E. DIST. OF N.Y. AND THE S. DIST. OF N.Y., LOCAL RULES OF THE UNITED STATES DISTRICT COURTS FOR THE SOUTHERN AND EASTERN DISTRICTS OF NEW YORK, http://www.nysd.uscourts.gov/rules/rules.pdf.

26. SHIRA A. SCHEINDLIN, INDIVIDUAL RULES AND PROCEDURES, http://www.notice-lawsuit.com/data/documents/judge-scheindlin-individual-rules-and-procedures.pdf.

27. FED. R. CIV. P. 56(b).

28. S.D.N.Y. CIV. R. 56.1(a).

29. SHIRA A. SCHEINDLIN, INDIVIDUAL RULES AND PROCEDURES, at 5, http://www.notice-lawsuit.com/data/documents/judge-scheindlin-individual-rules-and-procedures.pdf.

i. Framing the Legal Question

An apocryphal lawyer once said that he would gladly take either side of the case as long as he could pick the issues.[30] To a large degree, an issue statement provides the opportunity to do just that.

The lens through which a judge views a case can influence its outcome.[31] Not only have judges and legal scholars said as much, but this insight also has found vast support in the field of cognitive psychology and its work on the framing effect. Psychologists have learned, for instance, that people tend to avoid risk when a question is framed positively, but will accept greater risk if the same question is framed negatively.

Here's one example of what that means: Researchers asked participants in one study to choose a treatment option for an unusual disease breaking out in the United States that would kill 600 people. The first scenario presented two treatment options: A and B. Under treatment option A, 200 people would be saved. Under treatment option B, there was a one-third chance that all 600 people would be saved and a two-thirds chance that no one would be saved. Seventy-two percent of participants chose option A. The second scenario also presented two options: C and D. Under treatment option C, 400 people would die. And under treatment option D, there was a one-third chance that none will die and a two-thirds chance that everyone would die. Seventy-eight percent of participants—nearly the same number of participants as in the first scenario—chose option D.[32]

Do you see the problem here? With 600 people facing death, there is no logical difference between saving 200 people and having 400 people die. (There is also no mathematical difference between having one-third of the patients survive and two-thirds die.) But when the issue is framed as one of death tolls rather than one of survival rates, participants flipped their treatment option preferences. This effect has been demonstrated again and again when it comes to decision-making; an individual's choice is impacted by the way the question is framed.[33]

---

30. As Scalia and Garner point out, the quote has been attributed to Clarence Darrow, Rufus Choate, John W. Davis and others. ANTONIN SCALIA & BRYAN A. GARNER, MAKING YOUR CASE 83 (2008).

31. *Id.* at 83–84 ("If the court decides to answer the question you pose, it will probably reach the conclusion you urge"); *see also* RICHARD A. POSNER, LAW AND LITERATURE: A MISUNDERSTOOD RELATION 305 (1988); Frederick Schauer, *Do Cases Make Bad Law?*, 73 U. CHI. L. REV. 883, 897–98 (2006).

32. Amos Tversky & Daniel Kahneman, *The Framing of Decisions and the Psychology of Choice*, 211 SCI. 453, 453 (1981).

33. *See, e.g.*, Melissa A. Z. Knoll, *The Role of Behavioral Economics and Behavioral Decision Making in Americans' Retirement Savings Decisions*, 70 SOC. SECURITY BULL. 1, 2

There is no reason to believe judges or juries are any less susceptible to these sorts of cognitive biases, as demonstrated by a debate over the Supreme Court's decision in Griswold v. Connecticut. Consider this issue statement, slightly modified from the one included in that case:

> Whether Connecticut's laws prohibiting the distribution of contraceptives to married couples deprive those couples of liberty without due process of law in violation of the Fourteenth Amendment to the Constitution of the United States.[34]

The Supreme Court decided in the petitioner's favor, but Judge Richard Posner posited that the Supreme Court's decision in a similar case may not have been so clear-cut if the issue statement instead focused on the effect of such a rule on the state. He suggested the following question:

> [W]hether the state is constitutionally obligated to allow the sale of goods that facilitate fornication ... by making those practices less costly.[35]

Changing the focus of the question from the coercion of the petitioners to the coercion of the state frames the issue powerfully from the other side. By starkly framing the negative consequences of a ruling against the government, Posner flips the terms of the debate and potentially primes the Justices for a ruling in the state's favor. Your Issue Statements should aim for similar results.

ii. Selecting Key Facts

Once you have decided how to frame the legal question, you must select the facts to use to hint at the answer to that question. The crucial criteria here are accuracy, persuasive value, and, if possible, the capacity to further your theme. Say that you are drafting a motion for summary judgment on behalf of your client, a plaintiff in a breach-of-contract case. Your theme is that valid promises must be kept, and the facts show that the defendant was an outlier in not delivering his goods on time. Your Issue Statement could be:

(2010) (discussing how "simple changes in the way options are presented, considered, or arranged ... can have profound effects on the choices individuals ultimately make"), https://www.ssa.gov/policy/docs/ssb/v70n4/v70n4p1.html.

34. *See* Brief for Appellants at 3–4, Griswold v. Connecticut, 381 U.S. 479 (1965) (No. 496), 1965 WL 92619.

35. Richard A. Posner, Law and Literature: A Misunderstood Relation 305 (1988) (discussing *Eisenstadt v. Baird*, 405 U.S. 438 (1972)).

The defendant admits he failed to deliver fifty widgets by the agreed-upon date, costing the plaintiff thousands of dollars in lost revenue. While a thunderstorm had disrupted the power supply to the defendant's factory, other manufacturers in the area were able to complete their shipments on time. Is the defendant liable for breach of contract?

Here, the brief-writer picks facts that are undeniably true and also frame the issue favorably for her side. The key facts—the facts that win the case for the plaintiff—are the failure to deliver (showing the contract was breached) and the fact that other manufacturers continued their deliveries (showing the inexcusability of that breach). The defendant in the same case cannot deny that these facts are true. What he can do is focus on other facts that excuse this failure to deliver:

> Whether the defendant is excused from performance of the contract when he delivered fifty widgets only two days after the agreed-upon date after a thunderstorm knocked out power to his factory for over a week.

The facts that the defendant chooses to highlight paint a very different picture. Rather than a bumbling factory owner who was unable to meet his commitments when other manufacturers did, the defendant here appears heroic in the face of difficult circumstances. Emphasizing both the limited time difference between the expected date of delivery and actual delivery ("only two days") and the severity of the difficulties he faced ("knocked out power ... for over a week") changes the focus of the story from one of failure to one of triumph.

iii. Putting It All Together: Examples of Effective Issue Statements

An effective Issue Statement both frames the issue in favor of the client and includes facts that reflect the theme of the brief. However, it is no easy feat to manage both tasks, as an Issue Statement ideally spans only seventy-five words or less. The examples below, pulled from briefs filed by well-known advocates, succeed either by emphasizing key facts or by framing the issue in a particularly effective way.

Example 1:
Whether a person who receives a gift of money derived from drug trafficking, and uses that money to purchase real property, can assert

an "innocent owner" defense to civil forfeiture of real property under 21 U.S.C. 881(a)(6).[36]

This Issue Statement is of the facts-frame-the-issue variety. Rather than focusing the legal question on the harm to the client (as in the *Griswold*/Posner examples above), it uses specific details to show that the socially desirable result is a ruling in favor of the United States. The advocate highlights key facts—such as the money's drug-trafficking roots and property-purchasing end—to imply that an enormous loophole in forfeiture law could be created if a criminal defendant could avoid asset forfeiture simply by transferring illicitly-gained money to a friend to purchase property.

Notice that the Issue Statement does not state that assertion directly. The question is not: "Whether a person who uses a loophole in the civil forfeiture law to purchase real property can keep that property." That framing is ineffective because it relies on a legal conclusion—that these facts present a loophole in forfeiture law—rather than on the facts of the case.

Example 2:
Whether a Michigan law criminalizing the sale of beverages in almost every other State of the Union based on the beverages' packaging amounts to the extraterritorial regulation of commerce in violation of the Commerce Clause of the United States Constitution.[37]

This example relies more on framing than on facts to persuade, but both pieces still play important roles. This case involved a Michigan law requiring beverage manufacturers to create unique packaging for Michigan in an attempt to prevent people from purchasing containers in other states and redeeming them in Michigan. Noting that the Michigan law "criminalizes the sale of beverages in almost every other State" frames the legal question through the lens of the harmful consequences of the statute.

Opposing counsel looked at the question quite differently:

Michigan law requires that beverage manufacturers include a unique-to-Michigan mark on all beverage containers sold in Michigan with a

---

36. Brief for the United States at I, United States v. A Parcel of Land, Bldgs., Appurtenances and Improvements, Known as 92A Buena Vista Ave., Rumson, N.J., 507 U.S. 111 (1993) (No. 91-781), 1993 WL 445385, at *I. John Roberts, now Chief Justice of the Supreme Court, was part of the team from the Solicitor General's office that drafted this brief.

37. Brief of Appellant Am. Beverage Ass'n at 2, Am. Beverage Ass'n v. Snyder, 735 F.3d 362 (6th Cir. 2013) (No. 11-2097), 2011 WL 6146282.

104A deposit. Did the District Court correctly hold that this requirement is neither extraterritorial nor discriminatory under the dormant
Commerce Clause?[38]

The focus here is on the local aspects of the statute—a Michigan law, a unique-
to-Michigan mark, beverages sold in Michigan—and the ruling below, which
was in the state's favor. This framing aims to pull the judges back to Michigan's
side by emphasizing the favorable facts of the case.

b. Background: Statement of the Case

After introducing and framing the legal issue, most briefs then provide
the story of what happened, called the Statement of the Case (or, in some
jurisdictions, a Statement of Facts).[39] To tell this story well, you should do
more than string facts together into a cohesive narrative. Also raid the fiction
writer's toolbox to highlight your theme. Fact selection, plot, character and
setting all have crucial roles to play; we discuss each device in more detail
below.

i. Fact Selection

The first step in crafting a persuasive Statement of the Case is deciding which
facts to present. You know from your reading on objective writing that you
must include all legally significant facts, even those facts that help the other
side. To do otherwise is to put your credibility into question.

Once you have accounted for all the legally relevant facts, you now can pick
and choose what additional facts to present. When identifying these details,
think about your theme. Say you are pursuing a "don't trust 'em" theme in a
contract dispute case; you want the court to believe that your opponent is a
repeat bad actor. Your Statement of the Case should then include small details
that show the other side is unreliable. For example, it might not be legally significant that your opponent, a widget-maker, has failed to make deliveries on

---

38. Brief for Mich. Defendants-Appellees at 2, Am. Beverage Ass'n v. Snyder, 735 F.3d
362 (6th Cir. 2013) (No. 11-2097), 2012 WL 473429.

39. Check the rules governing your jurisdiction for information on what should be included here (and what this section should be called). In some jurisdictions, it is called a
"Statement of Facts," and it includes only facts; a different section, called a "Statement of
the Case," lays out procedural history. See, e.g., Tex. R. App. P. 38.1(d), (g). In other jurisdictions, both the factual and procedural backgrounds are introduced in a "Statement of
the Case." See Fed. R. App. P. 28(a)(6). For our purposes, we will follow the Federal Rules
of Appellate Procedure and call this section a "Statement of the Case."

time on several occasions in the past, but that detail indicates a pattern of failing to live up to promises. And it might not be legally significant that this widget-maker has a history of uncorrected building inspection violations, but that detail indicates a pattern of neglect.

What facts might you want to avoid? That the widget-maker was in a part of town that was much more susceptible to flooding than other widget-makers. That your client has a history of unreasonable enforcement actions against widget-makers. That your client had moved up the date of delivery and threatened to void the contract, despite the widget-maker's concerns about storms at that time of year.

Those details may be omitted, if they are not relevant to the legal questions in the case. They paint your client in a negative light and may elicit a judge's sympathy for your opponent. Generally, you should not bring them up unless and until your opponent does.

But as with all things in legal writing, there are exceptions to this rule. For example, if you are certain your opponent will raise a negative fact, you can enhance your own credibility and inoculate your client from the fact's most harmful aspects by disclosing it first.[40] When considering whether or how to disclose, evaluate the harm the fact would cause and whether you could possibly frame it positively. You can choose one of several paths:

(1) Ignore the negative fact. This strategy works best if the fact is a relatively minor one, something that would not sway a reasonable judge.

(2) Ignore it, mostly. Note that this fact is not legally significant and thus irrelevant. The downside to this strategy: If the fact is something truly troubling to a decision-maker's conscience or sense of justice, to simply say "pay no attention to this" sounds defensive and may do more harm than good—"nothing to see here" rarely works to inoculate against the harm of a bad fact.

(3) Fully disclose, but overwhelm the negative fact with positive facts. This strategy works best when the fact is both truly damaging and can be effectively offset. Put the adverse fact in a broader context or juxtapose it with positive facts. Take our fictional failure-to-deliver-widgets case. If you represented the widget-maker in that case, and you knew your opponent would mention your client's past building code violations, you could contextualize that fact by noting that the building inspector has since been fired for falsifying reports, or that the factory underwent an overhaul after those violations and has not had a ci-

---

40. *See* Kathryn M. Stanchi, *Playing with Fire: The Science of Confronting Adverse Material in Legal Advocacy*, 60 RUTGERS L. REV. 381, 426–27 (2008) ("[V]olunteering unfavorable information can work as a sword (to boost credibility, to transform from negative to positive) and a shield (to resist attack).").

tation since. But if you cannot effectively offset the fact, it may be to your advantage to tell the positive story and take the chance that your opponent will not raise the adverse fact.[41]

ii. Plot

Now that you have collected your key facts, you must connect those dots into a plot that furthers your theme.

A plot is a narrative arc with a beginning, middle, and end. Where the story begins, what action moves it forward, and how an end is reached all convey subtle messages of causation and blame to the reader. Place two actions next to each other, and the reader will assume one caused the other. Note the advantages your opponent reaped from the situation, and the reader will blame her for the harm that befell your client. Moreover, by paying careful attention to the structure of your story, you highlight certain details and downplay others, thereby advancing your theme. A Statement of the Case's plot is thus a crucial tool for pathos-based advocacy; the following paragraphs provide specific strategies for mastering this structure.

Narrative theorists contend that a plot begins with a "steady state," grounded in the legitimate ordinariness of things, that is disturbed by some "trouble." Efforts to fix the trouble result in either restoration of the original steady state or transformation into a new steady state.[42] Legal stories generally begin either with an explicit description of this steady state, which is particularly apt if the attorney asks for the restoration of that state, or with the trouble, which works best if the attorney is asking for transformation into a new steady state.

For example, the plaintiff in our widget dispute could begin his story like so:

> Plaintiff Steve McWidget was under a tight deadline. He had promised thirty widgets to a customer by July 15th, and he was unable to produce all those widgets in his factory alone. He decided to contract with another widget-maker to ensure an on-time delivery to this long-time client. After some extensive research, McWidget decided to contract with Defendant Widgets Galore. Defendant promised he could deliver fifteen widgets by July 14th.

---

41. For a more detailed look at the science behind when and how to rebut negative facts and adverse authority, see generally *id*.

42. *See* Anthony G. Armstrong & Jerome Bruner, Minding the Law 113–14 (2002); Philip N. Meyer, Storytelling for Lawyers 13 (2014) (citing *id*.).

Defendant missed that deadline. The widgets were not delivered
on July 14th. Or on the next day. Or the next.

These paragraphs cast the plaintiff as a reasonable, responsible businessman,
someone trying to do his best for a valuable client. It also introduces the steady
state, a contract that ensured timely delivery and happy customers. Until the
bottom fell out. From this beginning, it is clear that the attorney will ask for
the decision-maker to restore this steady state and enforce the contract.

If an attorney is instead asking for a new steady state—say, to be excused
from performance of the contract—then she generally will want to begin her
legal tale with the trouble. In this kind of story, "[r]ight from the opening
scene, the world (or at least the protagonist's world) needs fixing or lacks something important."[43] For example, our defendant widget-maker could begin his
story like this:

> The tempest rolled in unexpectedly in the evening hours, after all
> the employees of Widgets Galore had gone home for the night. The
> powerful and fast-moving thunderstorm, called a "derecho," dropped
> two inches of water and pummeled the factory walls and roof with
> seventy-mile-per-hour winds. An hour after the storm began, it
> ended, but the damage to Widgets Galore was done. A hole in the
> roof had let in so much rain that the floor of the plant was completely
> flooded. Power went out that night and was not restored until three
> days later. When owner Melvin Smith arrived on the scene, he knew
> that the plant would have to be shut down for at least one day, likely
> several.
>
> Smith immediately tried to contact Plaintiff Steve McWidget to let
> him know about the storm damage and the delay in delivery.
> McWidget did not respond to either of Smith's two emails. Smith also
> tried to contact McWidget by phone on five separate occasions, but
> he received no response.

Here, the defendant begins not with the contract, but with the trouble that
has upended the contract. This trouble calls for a new response, a change in
the steady state of contract enforcement: an excuse from performance.

The key when deciding whether to begin with the steady state or with the
trouble is to know where you want the case to end. From the first sentence of
these two examples, the outcome the party wants is clear. The plaintiff wants

---

43. Linda H. Edwards, *Once Upon a Time in Law: Myth, Metaphor, and Authority*, 77
Tenn. L. Rev. 883, 886 (2010).

to be restored; the defendant wants to avoid liability. Design the beginning of your Statement of the Case with this end goal in mind.

This introduction to the facts sets the stage and foreshadows the conclusion. The rest of your Statement of the Case should escalate the conflict. Consider each paragraph to be a scene in a movie. One scene follows the next, deepening the conflict as the plot moves forward.[44]

Let's look back to our widget breach-of-contract case for an example of how this could look. Assume you are representing the defendant and begin your Statement of the Case as written in the second sample above. Your next paragraph could then escalate the conflict by describing the complications that arose from the storm and McWidget's lack of communication:

> The day after the storm, Smith and his manufacturing team spent four hours inventorying the damage. The inch of water on the floor had evaporated overnight, but the wooden flooring was cracked and warped from the moisture. The stockpile of deliveries that was ready to go out on the truck that day sat on the floor by the garage doors. The hole in the ceiling where water had seeped in was directly over that spot. All twelve boxes set for delivery, and their contents, were completely destroyed; the electronic widgets due to Steve McWidget on that day no longer turned on when activated.
>
> Smith again called McWidget, his sixth phone call to the Plaintiff, to inform him of the damage. He left a message on McWidget's voicemail, but received no response.

These latter paragraphs provide further details about the extent of the damage done by the storm, as well as the plaintiff's failure to respond. Each paragraph focuses on a particular scene: the first paragraph above could be labeled "storm damage," the second "additional calls to McWidget." When crafting your own Statement of the Case, consider beginning by drafting a flowchart of the scenes that will form the backbone of your story. Then devote a paragraph to each scene.

When the conflict reaches its climax, the work of the Statement of the Case is complete. Legal stories are unique in that they have not yet ended; the decision-maker must conclude the tale and provide the redress or transformation. But a persuasive document should provide the path forward, hinting at the

---

44. *Cf.* Kenneth D. Chestek, *The Plot Thickens: Appellate Brief as Story*, 14 J. LEGAL WRITING INST. 127, 148 (2008) ("[T]he conflict drives the story and grabs the reader's attention, and the author reveals the conflict through the complicating incident in any story. The incident may be a series of incidents, one building upon another (rising action).").

proper ending that would resolve this dispute and impose order after the chaos of the story's events.[45]

One possibility for suggesting resolution is to note the steps the party has taken in the court system to have the issue resolved. For Statements of the Case that require inclusion of the procedural history, the last paragraph serves the dual purposes of including that history and proposing a possible resolution. For example,

> McWidget filed a complaint against Smith on October 1, 2014. For the past six months, the parties have engaged in extensive discovery, including multiple depositions of Smith. After discovery concluded, Smith filed this motion for summary judgment, asking the court to dismiss the case as a matter of law.

This conclusion does not explicitly say "rule in my client's favor," but, by noting where the case stands, it implicitly extends that invitation. Highlighting the lengthy discovery period also implies that the case has taken an unjust toll on Smith, and the judge has an opportunity to right that wrong by deciding in Smith's favor.

iii. Character and Setting

Plot provides the structure of your Statement of the Case, but it alone is not enough to constitute a compelling story. You must fill in that outline with specific, small details that bring those other key storytelling tools—character and setting—to life.

Character is a crucial aspect of a Statement of the Case because you are asking a court to impose a state-sanctioned harm on the opposing party, and human beings (including judges and juries) prefer to impose harms on those who deserve them. Take our contract case from above as an example. To rule in McWidget's favor would harm Smith because Smith would have to pay damages. To rule in Smith's favor would harm McWidget because McWidget has suffered losses for which he will not be compensated.

While a decision-maker may prefer to think of a court decision as dispensing justice or correcting wrongs, at its most basic it distributes (or redistributes) a harm that has occurred. And a judge or a jury does not want to impose harm on innocent individuals or entities. Thus, character plays a critical role in show-

---

45. Brian J. Foley & Ruth Anne Robbins, *Fiction 101: A Primer for Lawyers on How to Use Fiction Writing Techniques to Write Persuasive Facts Sections*, 32 RUTGERS L. J. 459, 477 (2001).

ing that your client is blameless (or at least less blame-worthy than your opponent).

To accomplish this task, you must provide details that illuminate your client's motivations or the traits that make her actions understandable or sympathetic. Here is one example of small, specific details making a large impact:

> Operating 365 days a year, 24 hours a day, the Red Dog Mine is the largest private employer in the Northwest Arctic Borough, an area roughly the size of the State of Indiana with a population of about 7,000.... Prior to the mine's opening, the average wage in the borough was well below the state average; a year after its opening, the borough's average exceeded that of the State.[46]

Here, then-advocate (now-Supreme Court Chief Justice) John Roberts uses specific details to show the benefits of the mining operation: It is the "largest private employer" in the borough and wages in the area increased after its opening. Notice that he does not tell his readers, "The Red Dog Mine has been an economic savior for the people of the borough." He instead uses the specific details about employment at the mine to subtly lead readers to that conclusion.

Setting can also be wrought through the use of finely tuned details. While less crucial than plot or character, setting can prove critical in certain kinds of legal stories. For instance, questions of whether a confession was coerced can rely heavily on the environment surrounding the detainee. In other circumstances, legal storytellers can use environments as explanations for the wrongdoing of a party; for example, an attorney might provide detail about the abusive home a criminal defendant grew up in.

A classic example of the difference details can make in setting a scene comes from the *Walker/Shuttlesworth* line of Supreme Court cases. These two opinions describe the exact same scene on the exact same evening (both written by Justice Potter Stewart), but the details paint very different pictures of the same event.

Example 1:
That night a meeting took place at which one of the petitioners announced that 'injunction or no injunction we are going to march tomorrow.' The next afternoon, Good Friday, a large crowd gathered in the vicinity of Sixteenth Street and Sixth Avenue North in

---

46. Brief for Petitioner at 9, Alaska Dep't of Envtl. Conservation v. E.P.A., 540 U.S. 461 (2004) (No. 02-658), 2003 WL 2010655.

Birmingham. A group of about 50 or 60 proceeded to parade along the sidewalk while a crowd of 1,000 to 1,500 onlookers stood by, 'clapping, and hollering, and (w)hooping.' Some of the crowd followed the marchers and spilled out into the street.[47]

Example 2:
On the afternoon of April 12, Good Friday, 1963, 52 people, all Negroes, were led out of a Birmingham church by three Negro ministers, one of whom was the petitioner, Fred L. Shuttlesworth. They walked in an orderly fashion, two abreast for the most part, for four blocks. The purpose of their march was to protest the alleged denial of civil rights to Negroes in the city of Birmingham. The marchers stayed on the sidewalks except at street intersections, and they did not interfere with other pedestrians. No automobiles were obstructed, nor were traffic signals disobeyed.... The spectators at some points spilled out into the streets, but the street was not blocked and vehicles were not obstructed.[48]

Compare the way each of these opinions describes the crowd. Example 1 details "50 or 60 proceeded to parade along the sidewalk while a crowd of 1,000 to 1,500 onlookers stood by, 'clapping, and hollering, and (w)hooping.'" The writer zooms in on those details that make the march seem disorderly, and a picture of a group on the verge of a riot is thus seared into the reader's mind. Example 2 zooms in on the peaceful aspects of the crowd by highlighting what it did not do: The marchers "stayed on the sidewalks," "did not interfere with other pedestrians," and did not obstruct automobiles or disobey traffic signals. A vision of an orderly march emerges.

One last point about the use of details: The facts you choose to highlight in your Statement of the Case must be in the factual record presented to the court. Unlike novelists or filmmakers, the legal storyteller must provide support for her factual statements. Thus, as we noted in our earlier chapter on fact development, attorneys may have to dig to find these kinds of details. And once found, they must be memorialized through testimony or other documentary evidence. The fact statement then must contain citations to these records. Credibility is of the utmost importance, and it is vital not to introduce or highlight facts that have no evidentiary foundation so as to avoid the appearance of exaggeration or fabrication.

---

47. Walker v. Birmingham, 388 U.S. 307, 310–11 (1967).
48. Shuttlesworth v. Birmingham, 394 U.S. 147, 148–49 (1969).

c. Summary of the Argument

Many courts require an Introduction or Summary of the Argument section that concisely lays out a brief's legal conclusions.[49] Even if the rules do not require such a section, include it. Many judges read this section first; some consider it the most important part of the brief.[50]

Your goals in this section are threefold: (1) to give the decision-maker a snapshot of your main legal theories, (2) to tie together your legal theories and theme, and (3) to provide a powerful reason why your side should prevail. All this should be accomplished in a small space: no more than two or three pages for the most complicated arguments. Most summaries can (and should) be less than a page. This is the place to survey the forest, not examine the bark of the trees.

When structuring a summary, consider breaking it down into two parts: a theme-based introduction and a paragraph-by-paragraph roadmap of each of your main legal theories. In the best summaries, these later paragraphs do more than simply repeat your point headings (and the Federal Rules of Appellate Procedure explicitly prohibit such a stock approach). Instead, intertwine your legal theories and theme to create compelling arguments in favor of your side.

As the first sentence of the first paragraph of your Summary is a key point of emphasis, use it to powerfully present your theme.[51] Below is one example of a theme-based introduction, drawn from the Summary of Argument in a copyright infringement case against Google for its book-searching service, Google Books:

> The essence of the fair use inquiry is whether the use at issue furthers copyright's goal of promoting science and the arts or whether it impedes that purpose. Google Books provides an unprecedented method for discovering books relevant to a reader's interests, revealing stories of human knowledge that would otherwise be difficult or impossible to find.... At the same time, Google Books does not displace book purchases or diminish incentives for authors to advance human knowledge by creating new works; to the contrary, it benefits authors

---

49. *See, e.g.,* Fed. R. App. P. 28(a)(7); Pa. R. App. P. 2118.

50. *See* Antonin Scalia & Bryan A. Garner, Making Your Case 80 (2008); Ruggero J. Aldisert, Winning on Appeal: Better Briefs and Oral Argument 184 (2d ed. 2003) (calling the summary the brief's "structural centerpiece").

51. *See* Judith D. Fischer, *Summing It Up with Panache: Framing a Brief's Summary of the Argument,* 48 J. Marshall L. Rev. 991, 999–1000 (2015).

by enabling readers to find books and by fostering the advance of knowledge and scholarship.[52]

The advocate begins the Summary with a high-level overview of the case—not the specific four-factor fair use test at issue, but the deeper policy reasons for the existence of the test. His theme is that Google Books is a breakthrough advancement for human knowledge, an outright societal good. The fair use inquiry was designed to protect exactly these kinds of society-enhancing uses of copyrighted works.

That theme then winds its way through the four fair use factors. The writer devotes a paragraph to summarizing his arguments on each. Here is one example:

> Google Books also has no adverse effect on the potential market for or value of the copyrighted work (the fourth factor). The analysis of this factor is straightforward because Google Books serves an entirely different market function than the original work—it enables users to discover books, not read them. Plaintiffs have produced no evidence that Google Books displaces book purchases; instead, by enabling readers and scholars to discover books, Google Books enhances book sales.[53]

Notice that the writer restates the theme of social benefit by reiterating the notion that Google Books allows readers to "discover" works. Moreover, the writer uses specific, concrete details to powerfully summarize his argument on this point. He writes of a "different market function" and then describes exactly what that function is. He points to the plaintiff's lack of evidence of harm to book sales.

When writing summaries for the first time, advocates tend either toward overgeneralization or oversummarization. An overgeneralized summary is too broad and vague to be useful. For example, compare this to the above summary in the *Authors Guild* case:

> The fourth factor is the effect of the use upon the potential market for or value of the copyrighted work. Google Books does not sell books and thus does not cause any injury to the copyright holder. Therefore, this factor weighs in Google Books' favor.

---

52. Brief for Appellee at 21–22, Authors Guild v. Google, Inc., 804 F.3d 202 (2d Cir. 2015) (No. 13-4829-cv), 2014 WL 3385748.

53. *Id.* at 24.

This Summary does little more than repeat the syllogism at the heart of the case. While such a statement may be an accurate summary of the legal argument for why your side wins, it does not provide the specific details that both allude to the theme of the case and persuade the judge that your legal arguments are well-founded.

The other mistake is to veer into too much detail. A Summary generally should not contain case citations. Cites to one or two of the absolutely critical cases may be included, but any more than that and the Summary becomes bogged down in the legal weeds. Moreover, it is not necessary to mention every single argument you will make in your argument section. Pick and choose your main arguments—the ones that form the backbone of your brief—and highlight those in the Summary. Your minor arguments can then be the icing on your Argument cake.

One possible effective conclusion for your Summary is to anticipate and defuse your opponent's theme. If you can rebut it quickly and definitively, do so here. This provides the knockout punch that wraps up your section and leaves your reader thirsty for the details of your legal arguments. For one example of this, look to the conclusion of the University of Texas' Supreme Court brief in support of its affirmative action program: "Abruptly reversing course here would upset legitimate expectations in the rule of law—not to mention the profoundly important societal interests in ensuring that the future leaders of America are trained in a campus environment in which they are exposed to the full educational benefits of diversity."[54]

Yet, if you have no such counterpunch at the ready and revisiting your theme will simply be repetitive, conclude with the last of your paragraphs discussing the main legal theories. This is exactly how the author of our Google Books sample above concludes.[55]

d. Argument

All of the previous sections—Issue Statement, Statement of the Case, Summary of Argument—accomplish crucial persuasive goals. Yet their main purpose is to prime a decision-maker for the main event, the Argument section.

What should be included in this section? The Federal Rules of Appellate Procedure demand that an advocate's arguments contain her "contentions and

---

54. Brief for Respondents at 22, Fisher v. Univ. of Tex., 133 S. Ct. 2411 (2013) (No. 11-345), 2012 WL 3245488.

55. Brief for Appellee at 24–25, Authors Guild v. Google, Inc., 804 F.3d 202 (2d Cir. 2015) (No. 13-4829-cv), 2014 WL 3385748.

the reasons for them, with citations...."[56] Simple enough, but this instruction provides little help to one who aims to elegantly persuade, who strives to craft powerful briefs that change minds.

Your grounding in legal reasoning—deductive, inductive, and analogical—will serve you well when you begin to craft persuasive arguments. The basic tenets of legal reasoning still hold true in a persuasive context, and the legal syllogism will be at the heart of your strongest arguments. But syllogisms—and the Rule-Application-Conclusion structure—are just the starting point. Your task now is to frame your arguments so that the decision-maker is convinced that a ruling in your favor is both demanded by the law and the right thing to do.

The sections below provide advice on ways to accomplish this goal.

i. Selecting and Using Authorities

Be thoughtful when you select the authorities to highlight in your brief. Research into any area of law will almost always turn up a multitude of relevant cases, statutes, regulations, treatises, or other authorities. Stuffing your brief with every authority you find will lead to glazed eyes and bored minds. Instead, discuss in the text only those authorities that are the most crucial, one or two per point made. Supporting authorities can be relegated to string cites (or, more controversially, footnotes).[57]

The choice of cases to use is made significantly easier when there is binding authority that directly addresses the legal question at hand. You must cite to these cases and generally will devote some time in your brief to discussing them, especially when that binding authority is to your advantage. On those happy days, highlight the favorable law at the beginning of the brief and remind the judge of this controlling precedent throughout.

But even when the law gods have smiled upon you, do not sacrifice your theme on the altar of legal authorities. A decision-maker should be told not only that she is legally compelled to do something, but also why it is the just outcome. Thus, your argument needs both a legal theory and a theme.

In his book on advocacy, Noah Messing highlighted this point well when he excerpted a motion to dismiss in which the law all pointed in the right direction,

---

56. FED. R. APP. P. 28(a)(8)(A).

57. *See* Rich Cassidy, *Bryan Garner Says: Put Your Citations into Footnotes*, ON LAWYERING (Mar. 3, 2014), http://onlawyering.com/2014/03/bryan-garner-says-put-your-citations-in-footnotes/ (mentioning the debate between Justice Scalia and Bryan Garner on whether citations belong in the main body of the text or rather in footnotes).

but the motion was denied.[58] In that case, the Child Citizenship Act offered a path to citizenship for foreign-born children of United States residents, but only until the child was eighteen years old. Laura Liston, the plaintiff in the case, was just past her eighteenth birthday. The plain terms of the statute appeared to bar her application for citizenship under this provision. Yet the government did little to mitigate the sense that the result in this case was unfair:

> While the law may admittedly operate harshly on some applicants, USCIS is simply not empowered to substitute more lenient requirements for those imposed by Congress. In a case dealing with a similar provision of the Child Citizenship Act ("CCA"), the Ninth Circuit has recognized that despite seemingly harsh results, the Act has firm and explicit age requirements that must be followed.[59]

To repeatedly mention that the ruling in the case is "harsh" would give most decision-makers pause. If the advocate had offset that concession with some reason why the result is warranted or just—the administrative ease of a clear law or the availability of other paths to citizenship for Liston—the result may have been more favorable. The government did eventually prevail; the court granted summary judgment on essentially the same grounds the government advocated for in this brief, but seven months after the court denied this motion to dismiss.[60]

When the law points to a certain outcome, the path is clear: rely on it heavily, and pair it with a compelling theme. But few cases are decided so easily. If the solution to the legal problem were obvious, the parties usually would have resolved the dispute before the courthouse steps. In most disputes that progress to lawsuits, no controlling authority clearly answers the questions raised. An advocate then must rely on persuasive authority to support her points. But when an advocate finds herself in that great grey zone of persuasive authority, which cases or statutes should she choose? And how many should she use?

First, avoid resting your affirmative arguments on authorities that rule against your side. For example, if you are arguing for a grant of a motion for

---

58. *See* NOAH A. MESSING, THE ART OF ADVOCACY 60–61 (2013).

59. United States' Memorandum of Authorities in Support of Motion to Dismiss at 9–10, Liston v. Chertoff, No. CV-06-0265-LRS, 2007 WL 2773829 (E.D. Wash. Sept. 21, 2007), 2007 WL 681178.

60. Liston v. Chertoff, No. CV-06-0265-LRS, 2008 WL 906732, at *3–4 (E.D. Wash. Apr. 1, 2008).

summary judgment, use cases where the motion was also granted. An advocate often becomes mired in quicksand when she analogizes to a case that has some favorable language but ultimately denies the summary judgment motion. If the facts of these two cases are as analogous as you say, a judge thinks to herself, why should I grant the motion if it was denied in the previous case?

Also, if your brief addresses multiple issues, and a non-binding precedent rules favorably on one of your legal arguments but unfavorably on another, do not rest your brief on it. If you must cite to such a case (perhaps because your opponent has already relied upon it), ensure you have a good reason why that case's analysis of the second argument does not doom your argument to a similar fate.

Of course, you will have to mention the cases that harm you. Your opponent will certainly do so, and the court is expecting to hear your reasons why those cases do not win the day. But only introduce those cases when distinguishing them. When crafting your affirmative points—the reasons why you win, rather than the reasons why you don't lose—rest those arguments on the firm foundation of favorable authority whenever possible.

Second, once you have found those favorable authorities, choose the most favorable from among them. Different considerations come into play here. The best cases apply the law of your jurisdiction and are factually analogous to your case. If your jurisdiction does not provide any cases that meet these criteria, then expand your search for persuasive authority to other jurisdictions until you have filled in all the legal gaps in your argument.

When searching outside your jurisdiction, though, ensure that the law of the persuasive jurisdiction is nearly identical to the law of the court you are petitioning. Few things are more harmful to an argument than a response brief that notes, oh so carefully, how the law in that circuit fundamentally differs from the law in this one.

Third, focus your fire. Do not make every possible argument for victory; present only those arguments that stand the strongest chances of success. No judge wants to read a kitchen-sink brief, and the multitude of arguments often work at cross-purposes, counteracting each other. Give the judge a select few reasons why your client wins.

Once you have winnowed down the legal authorities to the chosen few, buttress the arguments based on those authorities mightily. Perhaps one persuasive case is strongly analogous to your facts and has a favorable outcome. Excellent. Spend some time discussing this case. But include a string cite with similar cases to prove that the case you are relying on is not an outlier. Provide the public policy reasons why the outcome urged by this case is just and fair. And highlight the distinctions between your facts and the facts from the cases your opponent cites. All of these supporting beams bolster your argument so that it can withstand attack from your opponent.

ii. Framing Rules

As we noted in Chapter 3, rules are often malleable, particularly (though not exclusively) when rules develop through the common law. A rule can be framed either positively (it applies when ...) or negatively (it does not apply when ...). It can highlight the burden on the opposing party. It can be framed broadly to emphasize the wide spectrum of activities it covers or narrowly to highlight its applicability to only a specific set of circumstances. It can be stated so that it incorporates policy objectives, or it can be stripped clean of them. As an advocate, you can use these different frames to present the most favorable rule for your client.

Begin by stating the rule neutrally. For example, under the Federal Rules of Civil Procedure, summary judgment should be granted "if the movant shows that there is no genuine dispute as to any material fact and the movant is entitled to judgment as a matter of law."[61] If you were writing a memo analyzing whether a court would grant summary judgment, you would use that language as the rule in the first paragraph.

Next, examine that neutral rule from every angle. Look first to the cases interpreting the rule, particularly those cases that are decided in favor of your side. For example, cases interpreting the summary judgment standard have said that plaintiffs cannot merely rest on assertions to avoid summary judgment; they must do more. Your rule thus can focus on what plaintiffs need to show rather than the neutral summary judgment standard:

> Plaintiffs' burden in responding to this motion is to identify the "specific facts" that support his claim of an oral agreement. *Baughman v. Am. Tel. & Telegraph Co.*, 410 S.E.2d 537, 545–46 (S.C. 1991) ("Bald allegations" are insufficient to create a genuine issue of fact and defeat defense motion for summary judgment). Because they cannot identify any such facts, this motion should be granted as a matter of law. *See Anderson v. Westinghouse Savannah River Co.*, 406 F.3d 248, 260 (4th Cir. 2005).[62]

---

61. FED. R. CIV. P. 56(a).

62. Memorandum in Support of Defendants' Motion for Summary Judgment at 14, Trademark Props. v. A&E Television Networks, No. 2:06-cv-02195-CWH (D.S.C. Apr. 13, 2007).

This approach downshifts the legal rule from the broad general standard to the specifics of what a plaintiff needs to show to survive summary judgment in an oral contract case. The advocate has flipped the focus from what he needs to prove to win summary judgment to what his opponent needs to prove to avoid it.

Of course, if you represented the plaintiff in the above case, your focus would remain squarely on the summary judgment standard as laid out in the Federal Rules of Civil Procedure:

> To succeed on his motion for summary judgment, defendant must show no dispute of material fact in a case that is, at its core, a he said/she said dispute. *See* Fed. R. Civ. P. 56(a). Because it would be inappropriate for a court to decide the factual issues at the heart of the case at this stage, the motion for summary judgment should be denied.

Yet, even here, when the language of the standard is favorable to your client, it is not presented neutrally. This opening emphasizes the "dispute of material fact" aspect of the standard and immediately makes the point that this case is nothing more than such a dispute.

If flipping the rule will not work, another option is to broaden or narrow the scope of the rule. Use a narrow rule when you argue that the activity at issue falls outside the rule's boundaries, and a broad one when arguing that the rule captures the disputed actions. Here is an example of each:

> *Narrow rule:* A search incident to arrest is a narrow exception to the warrant requirement; if intended to prevent the destruction of evidence, such searches must be conducted during or immediately after the arrest.
> *Broad rule:* A search incident to arrest ensures that the government can prevent destruction of evidence, as long as such searches occur within a reasonable time frame.

These examples each use different framing techniques: context and word choice. The "narrow" rule emphasizes the search incident to arrest as an exception to the usual requirement that police obtain a warrant before a search. This "exception to the general rule" frame provides the broader context of the rule and primes the decision-maker to carefully scrutinize the circumstances of this case so that the exception remains limited. The words the advocate chooses to describe the time frame under which such a search is allowed— "during or immediately after" an arrest—continue this theme of a narrow exception.

The "broad" rule focuses instead on the policy reasons for the existence of this exception: the prevention of the destruction of evidence. By highlighting this reason for the rule, the advocate invites the decision-maker to consider whether the search in this case did prevent the destruction of evidence, thus achieving the goal of the rule. The advocate's word choice for the timeline of the search—it must be "reasonable"—is more of a standard than the "during or immediately after" rule and thus enables the judge to focus on whether the goals of the rule were achieved.

iii. Applying Rules

The application of these framed rules also must be persuasive. Just as with objective legal analysis, your analogies and distinctions should include the facts, reasoning, and holding of the precedent, and you should match up the facts of the precedent with the facts of your case. But in persuasive writing, the analogies or distinctions must be as tight and crisp as possible. The point of every analogy is to prove that the precedent compels a result in your client's favor.

To do this well, use parallel structure to align facts from the precedent and facts from the current case. In objective writing, a writer will often describe the facts, reasoning, and holding of the precedent before moving into the current set of facts. A persuasive approach will meld that information with the facts of the current case.

Let's look at this technique in action. First, here is an example of an objective rule application:

> *Objective:* In *Reid*, officers were unreasonable to assume that a third party who answered the door had apparent authority over the defendant's residence, when he could not identify who owned the car parked in the driveway. *Reid*, 539 F.3d at 57. Similarly, Cooper was unreasonable to assume that Florrick's short-term renter status gave her apparent authority over Crawley's computer, when Florrick could not identify the correct password needed to use it.

Here is the same analogy, framed persuasively. Note how the writer below intermixes the facts from the precedent (in plain font) with facts from the current case (in bold).

> *Persuasive:* In *Reid*, officers were unreasonable when they assumed that a third party who simply answered the door, **like Florrick did here**, had apparent authority over defendant's residence. *Reid*, 539 F.3d at 57. The third party in *Reid* could not name the owner of the

car in the driveway, **just as Florrick could not name the password that unlocked the computer in the living room.** *Id.*

The end result is a crisp and persuasive analogy that overlaps the facts of the precedent with the facts from the current case. The reader knows exactly why officers in this case were unreasonable, just as they were in the precedential case.

iv. Crafting Policy Arguments

Case law, statutory text, and other legal authorities will provide you with the rules that govern your particular factual circumstance. As an advocate, you frame and apply those rules, using the techniques outlined above. But, often, the rules alone are insufficient to persuade, particularly when the opposing party has equally compelling rule-based arguments. In such cases, the judge turns to her "can't helps"—common sense, ideological persuasion, sense of moral rightness—to decide the case.

The best advocacy therefore rests on more than the application of rules to facts. It also shows the judge that your proposed outcome is in some way better than an outcome for the opponent. What exactly constitutes a "better" result is a deep and difficult question, and the answer will vary from case to case. As a starting point, ask yourself two questions: (1) how does my proposed outcome fulfill the goal of the legal rule? and (2) how would a ruling in my favor benefit society generally (or how would a ruling in my opponent's favor cause societal harm)? The answers to these questions form the foundation of your policy arguments.

Before we delve into these two kinds of policy arguments, first a word about how to present these arguments: subtly. Novice writers often think there should be some separate section of a brief devoted to a policy argument. Not usually. Unless there is good reason to include a separate section on policy (perhaps because you are interpreting a new statute that no judge has yet ruled on), these arguments are more effective when woven into the legal arguments you make throughout the brief. They provide additional support for your rule-based outcome.

Moreover, policy arguments should be supported by authority of some kind. It is not enough that it is a moral good (in your eyes) that your side wins. There must be some reason for a court to trust your assessment. This reason ideally comes in the form of a citation to another court's decision, but if diligent research turns up no such authority, turn instead to secondary sources like treatises or journal articles. The key is to find support for the conclusions you propose.

The example below highlights a policy argument in the purpose-behind-the-rule vein. The advocate argues that Google Books' copying and archiving of copyrighted works is protected by fair use, in part because this use would have no adverse effect on the market for the authors' works. The brief's argument on this factor of the fair use test analogizes to Supreme Court precedent on this question before concluding with this paragraph:

> Ultimately, the fourth factor is focused on "the author's incentive to create." *Sony Corp of Am. v. Universal City Studios, Inc.*, 464 U.S. 417, 450 (1984). "[A] use that has no demonstrable effect upon the potential market for, or the value of, the copyrighted work need not be prohibited in order to protect" that incentive. *Id.* Plaintiffs have offered no meaningful evidence that any author would be deterred from creating a new work as a result of Google Books' fair use, and there is no reason why a service that only enables readers to *discover* books would deter authors from writing them.[63]

With this paragraph, the advocate takes a step back from the comparisons to precedent and refocuses the court on the purpose behind the adverse effect rule. As the author states (and supports with a citation to a Supreme Court case), the goal of the rule is to protect "the author's incentive to create." Google Books does not deter authors from creating; therefore, the goal would not be furthered by a ruling in favor of the plaintiffs. This subtle introduction of the policy argument thus supports the rule-based reason why Google Books should prevail on this factor.

Additional policy support for an outcome can often be found in the impact a ruling will have on the judiciary or other systems of government. One subcategory of this kind of argument is the institutional competence policy argument. Advocates will often argue that it simply is not the court's job to meddle in specific kinds of cases because of the negative effects such meddling will have. Here is one example of an argument of this type:

> Moreover, it is contrary to the public interest to create a precedent that rewards drug users for ignoring a sports league's decisions by merely alleging procedural deficiencies, without providing any evidence that their respective urine samples did not contain illegal drugs. For good reason, courts are reluctant to second-guess a private sports organization's internal rules and decision making for fear of becoming "mired down in ... the 'dismal swamp'" of the organization's activity, of which "only [it] can speak competently." *Crouch v. Nat'l*

---

63. Brief for Appellee at 50, Authors Guild v. Google, Inc., 804 F.3d 202 (2d Cir. 2015) (No. 13-4829-cv), 2014 WL 3385748.

Ass'n for Stock Car Auto Racing, Inc., 845 F.2d 397, 403 (2d Cir. 1988). As this Court has recognized, judicial second-guessing after a plaintiff failed a drug test would lead to a situation where "injunctions would be routinely sought in drug discharge cases." *Guerra*, 942 F.2d at 275.[64]

Notice how the advocate in the example above lays out his argument in three steps: (1) he concludes that a ruling for his opponent is contrary to the public interest, (2) he shows that courts have been reluctant in the past to interfere in this area, and (3) he illustrates the specific negative consequences that would result if courts disregarded this reluctance. Both (2) and (3) are supported by cites to cases that have highlighted similar concerns in past situations. But while the case cited for (2) is focused on the specifics of "private sports organizations," it does not involve drug testing. And the case cited for (3) is a drug testing case that involves the Army, not a "private sports organization." Only by putting together these two cases can the advocate support the conclusion that the court should stay out of the business of second-guessing drug testing by private organizations.

As the above examples show, policy arguments can be difficult to craft and often require advocates to draw on cases or other authorities that may not factually align with the circumstances of the pending case. But when crafted effectively, these kinds of arguments can provide crucial supplemental support to rule-based persuasion.

v. Defusing Counterarguments

Litigants generally only pursue cases where they have valid arguments to make.[65] As an advocate, you may (and likely will) believe that your client should win her case, but that rarely means that your adversary is bereft of strong points in her favor. To shield your arguments from these slings and arrows, you must thoroughly counter your opponent's strongest points. This section discusses some techniques for accomplishing that goal.

---

64. Brief for Defendants-Appellants at 39, Mayfield v. Nat'l Ass'n for Stock Car Auto Racing, Inc., No. 09-1759 (4th Cir. Sept. 8, 2009), 2009 WL 2876302.

65. Of course, examples of exceptions to this rule abound. However, the federal courts, and most jurisdictions, require attorneys to sign papers submitted to courts, attesting that the arguments made are nonfrivolous. *See, e.g.*, FED. R. CIV. P. 11(b)(2) ("By presenting to the court a pleading, written motion, or other paper … an attorney or unrepresented party certifies that to the best of the person's knowledge, information, and belief, formed after an inquiry reasonable under the circumstances: … the claims, defenses, and other legal contentions are warranted by existing law or by a nonfrivolous argument for extending, modifying, or reversing existing law or for establishing new law; ….").

First, remember that the best defense is a good offense. Novice writers will often attempt to tear down their adversary's arguments before fully making their own. Avoid this urge. No matter how problematic your adversary's arguments are, your brief will look defensive if you bring the fight to their turf. Make your affirmative points before defusing the counterarguments.

Relatedly, when you turn to the counterarguments, avoid making your adversary's arguments for him, e.g., "Defendant argues that the bank examiner privilege bars production because these documents were produced by a bank." Instead, begin by concluding that your opponent's argument is wrong:

> The "bank examiner privilege" does not bar production here. BOC failed to produce a privilege log, which deprived Plaintiffs of a meaningful opportunity to evaluate the assertion of the privilege. The bank examiner privilege in any event belongs to the bank examiner, *Overby v. U.S. Fid. and Guar. Co.*, 224 F.2d 158, 163 (5th Cir. 1955); cannot be claimed by a private party, *id.*; is limited in scope; and can be outweighed by other interests where the documents sought are highly relevant, there is a lack of available other evidence, and serious issues are raised by the claims that outweigh the interest in candor between regulators and regulated parties. *Schreiber v. Sav. Bancorp, Inc.*, 11 F.3d 217, 220–21 (D.C. Cir. 1993). In a matter involving terrorist financing and a bank that is majority-owned by its regulator (the Chinese government), these factors favor the production of information.[66]

The advocate here wastes no time explaining the opponent's argument. He simply concludes that it fails and uses the follow-up sentences to provide the specific legal rules that show the privilege does not apply in these circumstances. He concludes by applying those rules to the facts of this case—terrorist financing and a bank owned by its regulator—to conclude that the information should be produced. Taken as a whole, it is a classic deductive reasoning paragraph, just flipped from an affirmative conclusion to a negative one.

The advocate in the next example uses slightly different tactics to achieve a similar result:

> Veldhoen's and Broekhoven's assertion that the regulations somehow contract the jurisdiction Congress has assigned to the Coast Guard is

---

[66]. Plaintiffs' Memorandum of Law in Support of Their Motion to Compel Production of Documents at 9, Wultz v. Bank of China Ltd., 910 F. Supp. 2d 548 (S.D.N.Y. 2012) (No. 11 Civ. 1266 (SAS)), 2012 WL 8502942.

a red herring. The regulation on which they rely, 46 C.F.R. §4.03-1(a), was promulgated prior to the passage of section 6101(e). The regulation thus does not purport to interpret section 6101(e) or any terms within it.[67]

This paragraph adopts a similar deductive organizational structure, but the first sentence presents a different tone. It may seem at first glance that this advocate is making her opponents' arguments for them, but this is not the case. Examine the way the advocate characterizes those arguments—"that the regulations *somehow* contract the jurisdiction"—to make them seem unserious. She then notes that the argument itself is a red herring. Referring to your adversary's argument can work well if you do not take it at face value; instead, frame it so that it is favorable to your side, just as you do with your affirmative points.

Second, think carefully about which counterarguments are strong enough that they require lengthy rebuttals and which can be disposed of quickly. Arguments that rest on controlling authority pose the direst threat to your position and generally should be carefully deconstructed. Even in an opening brief—before you know what arguments the other side will make—you must notify the court of negative controlling authority, while simultaneously showing why that authority does not doom your case. The "bank examiner privilege" excerpt above provides a good example of how to do this; the advocate knew that an argument could be made that the privilege applied to this situation. He thus spent a section of his brief showing the court why that common law rule, which had been adopted in the Second Circuit, did not bar the production of documents in that case.

Counterarguments that rest on persuasive authority can also be harmful, especially if that authority is factually analogous or particularly well-reasoned. After you have completed your research, there are usually at least one or two authorities that keep you up at night, that expose the holes in your own analysis. Those authorities will be the source of the questions that will be in the decision-maker's mind as she reads your document. A strong brief will anticipate and answer those questions.

Third, recognize when you have already won the battle. Minor persuasive authorities—the kinds of cases that are side notes, not the heart of an opponent's case—are rarely worth lengthy rebuttals. Simply making your affirmative points as strongly as possible can often do much of the work of defusing an opponent's potential arguments grounded in these kinds of authorities.

---

67. Brief for Appellees at 22, Veldhoen v. U.S. Coast Guard, 35 F.3d 222 (5th Cir. 1994) (No. 93-3788), 1994 WL 16065680.

vi. Pointheadings

As your mind swirls through the jumble of arguments and counterarguments, the plain language of legal rules and their broader purpose, the framing of rules and conclusions, confusion might abound. If you simply throw every one of your ideas and arguments into your brief, confusion will fester in the mind of your reader as well. Effective pointheadings impose order on chaos and help give your brief structure and sequence.

There are two types of pointheadings: main headings, which are the reasons why your side wins, and sub-headings, which provide another layer of detail and nuance to the legal conclusions reached in the main headings. The below headings are examples of main headings; each one reaches a legal conclusion and provides an independent ground for a ruling in the party's favor.[68]

   I. **The motion to dismiss should be granted because plaintiff can point to no facts supporting his claim of an oral agreement.**

   II. **The motion to dismiss should also be granted because the complicated contract plaintiff describes needs to be in writing to be enforceable.**

Perhaps you have multiple specific arguments to make in support of your conclusion that plaintiff has not alleged sufficient facts to survive a motion to dismiss. The sub-headings provide those more detailed descriptions of the arguments:

   I. **The motion to dismiss should be granted because plaintiff can point to no facts supporting his claim of an oral agreement.**

      A. *Plaintiff has sworn to three different versions of the events leading to the alleged contract formation.*

      B. *In none of these versions does plaintiff allege an acceptance.*

These sub-headings provide an additional layer of specificity and highlight the concrete arguments the defendant will make to support his claim that the plaintiff has not alleged facts supporting his claim. First, the fact that the plaintiff has sworn to three different versions of events indicates that he cannot keep his story straight. Second, even if the plaintiff could keep his story straight, none of the stories he told contained the required acceptance of an offer.

---

68. Generally speaking, main headings should be the independent reasons why your side prevails. If you have three reasons why you win, each one should get its own heading. If, however, there is only a single reason why your side wins—if there's only one legal issue that has been appealed, for example—then your main headings could be the separate factors that are considered under that one legal issue.

Each level down, from the main headings to the sub-headings, to any sub-sub-headings and beyond, should provide an additional layer of specificity. Headings work best when the main headings and the sub-headings can be connected to one another with a "because." Why can plaintiff point to no facts supporting his claim? Because he's sworn to three different versions of events. And because he has not alleged an acceptance. These sub-headings thus do not rest on generalities, but provide the specific facts—e.g., "three different versions of events"—that win the case.

The temptation here will be to stuff too much information into the point-headings, but resist the urge. Just as Questions Presented and Summaries of the Argument benefit from a judicious hand, so too do pointheadings. Include only the most crucial details here. For example, an advocate could have drafted something like the following in lieu of the above heading "*Plaintiff has sworn to three different versions of the events leading to the alleged contract formation*":

> A. *In Plaintiff's Complaint, he said the deal was made in New York; in his deposition, he said it was made over the phone; in his interrogatories, he said it was made in South Carolina. Not all of these stories can be true, and therefore the motion to dismiss should be granted.*

This pointheading lends itself to skimming because it contains too many details (the discrepancies between the stories) and repeats information included in the main heading (that the motion to dismiss should be granted). Limit your pointheadings to a line or two. If you find yourself exceeding that space, break that pointheading down into sub-headings. The first sentence of the heading above could be broken down into three sub-headings; that approach would be much more readable than trying to jam too much information into a single pointheading.

e. Conclusion

In a brief, a conclusion need only request relief from the court. You do not need to summarize your main points or rehash your arguments. The key to success here is to know exactly what you want the court to do. Deny the motion? Remand the case? Overturn the statute as unconstitutional? Whatever it is, clearly state that request in a line or two:

> For the foregoing reasons, the judgment of the district court should
> be reversed and summary judgment entered for the defendant.

Simple and to the point; this is all you need in this final section of your brief.

Index